Extinct animals of the British Isles

Justin Gerlach

© Justin Gerlach
2014
ISBN: 978-1-326-08603-9

http://islandbiodiversity.com/jg.htm

Contents

Introduction	5
Scarce animals of remote places	11
Shrinking forests	15
Draining the swamp	27
Dig for victory	39
Over the edge	51
Urban sprawl	59
Enigmas and exceptional cases	61
Rewilding – turning back the clock or tinkering?	75
List of extinct animal of Britain	79
References	85
Index	89

Introduction

The landscape of the British Isles is shaped by human activity; from farmland to moorland no part of the islands is truly natural. With thousands of years of such modification it is not surprising that many animal species have been lost. The exact number of extinctions is unknown as many may have disappeared before anyone recorded their presence. From what we do know around 136 species have become extinct, although a small number of these have recolonised the islands again, or been reintroduced. Of these 136 animals thought to have become extinct in Britain in historical times, 7 are mammals, 12 birds, 1 frog and 2 fish. The remaining 114 are invertebrates.

In identifying the extinctions caused by human activity it is necessary to determine when human impacts first started. In the British Isles this is surprisingly difficult as the geography has changed extensively and this has led to a long, but erratic human history.

The British Isles can be considered to have taken their present form as an archipelago of islands somewhere between 7,600 and 5,800 years ago. At this time the last Ice Age had come to an end and rising sea-levels had cut through the land bridges between the islands and the European mainland. Ireland had already been cut off from the rest of the British Isles when the Irish Sea had flooded 5,000 years earlier. This means that there was a narrow window of time in which animals could colonise the islands, between the retreat of the ice sheets and the flooding of the waterways.

Dating human occupation of the islands is less clear-cut. The earliest remains of our ancestors in Britain date back to around 900,000 years ago as indicated by remains of *Homo hiedelbergensis.* These retreated before the advancing ice, but returned briefly in warmer times around 400,000 years ago. The next time the islands were habitable was 230,000 years ago, by which time the human species had evolved into the Neanderthals, *Homo neanderthalensis.* Their colonisation was not very successful and the small population seems to have disappeared within 50,000 years. Our own species, *Homo sapiens*, does not appear in the islands until around 42,000 years ago. These seem to have been only temporary colonisations, with the repeated expansion of ice sheets forcing humans down into southern Europe. Permanent occupation did not happen until around 6,000 years ago. At this point in the late Stone Age (Neolithic) humans moving into Britain left behind evidence of agriculture and permanent settlement areas. Since then the islands have been shaped by human hands, and not by ice.

Even without the impact of humans, there have always been extinctions of animals and plants due to chance, catastrophic events and changing environments. The early natural extinctions are known now only from fossil remains. From these we can see that during the Ice Ages alternating periods of warm and cold conditions led to repeated invasions and extinctions of different species. In the warm interglacial periods there were temporary colonisations of species we now associate only with Africa: lions, hyenas and hippos for example. When the cold returned these species died out, to be replaced by bison, wolverines, reindeer, lemmings, mammoths and woolly rhinos. Some warm climate species invaded Britain shortly before the flooding of the North Sea and English Channel. These were then isolated as climates cooled once more. An example of these is the European pond turtle which survived in East Anglia until 3,000 BC.

If the history of the British Isles is taken to date from the complete isolation of the islands around 6,000 years ago, the last set of cold-adapted species were present from that point. Some had already disappeared: Arctic lemming, northern rat-vole, narrow-headed vole, pika, saiga, steppe lemming, woolly mammoth, woolly rhinoceros, tarpan, Irish elk, wolverine and cave lion were already extinct. Some cold-adapted species clung on: the northern vole (until 1,500 BC), root vole (1,500 BC) and the elk (1,400 BC). Although the elk was certainly hunted by Stone Age people it is likely these species would have died out due to climatic changes, irrespective of human activity.

The **aurochs** *Bos primigenius*, the ancient European wild cow, marks the last of the ancient extinctions. This seems to have died out around 1,000 BC (the most recent reliably dated remains being from 1,245 BC from Charterhouse Warren Farm). It was a forest cow, so could have been affected by loss of habitat in the Bronze Age, or hunting. Agricultural settlement probably reduced forest from 3,000 BC and the arrival of Iron Age Celts in 400 BC saw a rapid expansion of large-scale clearance and coppice. By Roman times the great forests had been lost. Despite this increase in the rate of deforestation there are no records of lost animals from Iron Age times (750BC-43AD).

By 1,000 BC the fauna of the islands seems to have stabilised, with the loss of those that found the climate of the islands either too warm or too cold. Now the main cause of extinctions was the environmental change caused by the increasing human population.

Identifying the extinct species of the British Isles is not as easy as it may first appear. Having defined a starting point of 1,000 BC, a species should either be present or absent. However, determining whether or not a species is

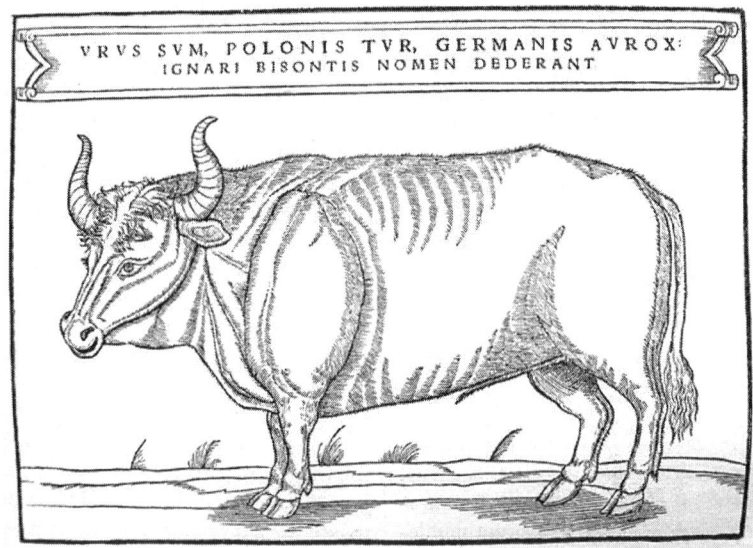
Aurochs drawn by Sigismund von Herbersetin in 1556

absent is far from simple. The larger species, such as bears and wolves should be obvious, but the vast majority of animals are small, inconspicuous invertebrates. There are several species that have been listed as extinct, only to be found many years later. Some of these were rare species that were overlooked, and were not extinct after all. Others may have been genuine extinctions but recolonised and managed to re-establish themselves.

Several **sawflies** are known in Britain only from single or questionable specimens from the 19th century: *Cimbex quadrimaculatus* near Salisbury, *Corynis crassicornis* near Bristol, *Corynis obscura* in Lincolnshire, *Megalodontes cephalotes* near Bristol and Plymouth, and *Strongylogaster filicis* from an unknown site. There are many other insects known from isolated records. Some may be misidentified or mislabelled. One such case is the **willow clytra beetle** *Clytra laeviuscula* which was reported from south England and Scotland in 1895, although it was not included in the major listing of beetles from the 18th century. It was reported to be not uncommon in Caledonian pine and birch woodland, and chalk grassland. The contradictory evidence of its abundance and its southern European distribution suggest that this may have been a misidentification for the widespread and not uncommon *C. quadripunctata*.

Some apparent extinctions may not really represent British species. They could be temporary introductions, as may be the case with the scattered old records of the eastern Mediterranean **scarab beetle** *Pleurophorus caesus*. The most recent record (in 1997) was definitely introduced, being found in imported celery in a supermarket. Some may have been escapes of captive animals, such as the records of the **scarce swallowtail butterfly** *Iphicles podalirius* between 1710 and 1822, the **hermit butterfly** *Chazara briseis* in 1938 and the **Niobe fritillary** *Argynnis niobe* between 1851 to 1892. Deliberate introductions are thought to be the cause of the isolated records of **Weaver's fritillary** *Boloria dia* (Warwickshire 1800s, Berkshire 1857, Surrey 1872, Kent 1876, Hampshire 1887, Suffolk 1899 and Gloucestershire 1907).

It is also difficult to be certain that a small invertebrate is actually extinct and there are several examples of rediscoveries. The **leaf beetle** *Galeruca laticollis* was thought to be extinct in Britain for most of the 20th century. It was recorded from marshes such as Whittlesea Mere in Cambridgeshire and finally at Wheatfen Broad, Surlingham. However it may have survived, overlooked in marshes or have recolonised from Europe for it reappeared in Wheatfen Broad in 1996. Its decline and apparent disappearance were probably due to the drainage of the meres throughout much of the 19th and 20th centuries. The main locality, Whittlesea Mere, was the second largest English lake but was drained in the 1850s. This was the last of the great meres to be drained, leaving just small patches of marsh and lake in largely agricultural land. The protection and restoration of some of these remnants such as Wicken Fen in Cambridgeshire

Weaver's fritillary after Morris 1853

and parts of the Norfolk Broads, may have allowed relict populations of the rare animals to survive and to re-establish themselves.

Some species should have been easy to find, such as the **orange-shouldered blister beetle** *Sitaris muralis*, a rare but highly distinctive black and yellow beetle, associated with old walls. In Britain it was found in southern England, most from one wall in Cowley, Oxford. Since the 1940s there had been very few sightings, with a long gap in records after 1969 and it was thought to be extinct. However, in 2000 it was found in Welling, Kent and in 2010 some were found in an old brick wall in Brockenhurst.

Other species have always been sparsely recorded: the **ground beetle** *Scybalicus oblongiusculus* was first recorded in Britain in 1878 in chalk grassland in Dorset (near Portland) and scattered sites from there to St Aldhelm's Head. It was last recorded there in 1951 and thought to be extinct. A puzzling record was made in Kew Gardens in 1998. In 2000 it was found in Ebbsfeet in Kent and in Essex in 2002. The lack of records between 1951 and the end of the century would appear to be due to the restricted range of the species, being found only in small habitat patches near the south coast.

In some cases the reappearance of supposedly extinct species seems to be due to recolonisation. The **small ranunculus moth** *Hecatera dysodea* was relatively common in the south-east of Britain until its extinction by the early part of the 20th century. There were no 20th century records after 1937; however in the last few years it has become re-established in a small area of Kent and Essex, around the Thames. It is often associated with allotments and is now expanding quite rapidly north and westwards.

Orange-shouldered blister beetle from Curtis 1824-39

Scarce animals of remote places

Some of the extinct species appear to have been rare in Britain throughout history. They are known from legends and folk tales, a few records and even fewer specimens.

Old bones show that **Eurasian lynx** *Lynx lynx* were definitely present throughout Britain in prehistoric times, but their more recent history is clouded in uncertainty. It had been thought that they disappeared 4,000 years ago due to climate change, but radio carbon dating of bones show that some lived in Scotland 1,770 years ago and in the Craven area of northern Yorkshire possibly as recently as 750 years ago, approximately 1250 AD.

Although these bones show that lynx were definitely present in Britain in historical times there are no good written records of them. Some words and texts may suggest lynx, specifically hunting of lynx in the Lake District in the 7th century and in Scotland until the late Mediaeval period, but these are fairly ambiguous. Lynx seem to have been rare throughout recorded history, probably because of the loss of the forests they are associated with and the precipitous decline in deer numbers in the Mediaeval period.

It has been suggested that reintroduction of the lynx could be appropriate in Scotland and northern England although in the modern landscape populations would be likely to remain low: estimated at just 500 animals, compared to a probable 7,000 during Stone Age times.

Even more enigmatic is the **capercaillie** *Tetrao urogallus*. This became a rarity in Britain so long ago that there are no proper records of established populations. It is known as a British bird from bones found in Yorkshire and Durham and a very small number of written references. The bones from Yorkshire were reported from Roman remains in the Victoria Cave at Settle, but how they were identified is unknown. Those from Durham were found in the Teesdale Cave by James Backhouse in the 1880s. Backhouse reported finding 'a vast quantity of mammalian and other animal remains…' None of the material found was dated but it is speculated to be around 2500 years old, based on dating of nearby ancient sites. Among the bones were several identified as capercaillies, although it is probable that only one could be identified with certainty: the humerus of a male, which would be larger than that of any other grouse. The numerous fragments of bones ascribed to females could have been large black grouse.

The first written record of a capercaillie is supposed to be the 'wode-hennes' being paid in rent to the Bishop of Durham in the 14th century. Such a rent was also exacted from Thomas de Missenden by Henry, Duke of Lancaster in 1360. This was for the Manor of Somborne in Hampshire, far from any remotely suitable capercaillie habitat. However, in Middle English a 'woodhen' was actually rent for access to a wood, paid in a quantity (a 'hen') of grain, so both these records can be disregarded.

There is a reference to the capercaillie in Hector Beothius's 'History of Scotland' in 1526, but without any details and in 1578 Bishop Lesley refers to capercaillies around Lochaber, the first specific locality.

Capercaillie by Walter Heubach (1865–1923)

In 1618 'caperkellies' were served to the guests of Lord Erskine (in Taylor's 'Visit to the Brea of Marr'). King James VI's laws of 1621 include protection of "powties, partrikes, moore foulles, blakcoks, gray hennis, termigantis, quailzies, capercailzies…" In 1651 one was apparently sent to King Charles II of England by the Laird of Glenorchy. The King 'accepted it weel as a raretie, for he had never seen any of them.' It was apparently still present at Glen Morison and the Chisholms in 1769 according to Pennant who gave a first hand account of a sighting.

In Ireland there are mentions in a few documents, but all are second-hand and after 1760 they had apparently all gone.

These imprecise and sparse records suggest that the capercaillie was always a rare bird in Britain. Its extinction seems to have occurred in the late 1700s as Stephens in Shaw's 'General Zoology' reports that Montagu was present when one was killed at Loch Lomond in about 1785, but Montagu himself never recorded this, so it is a little uncertain. Its loss was probably as a result of forest loss and hunting.

One was supposed to have been killed in about 1830 near Clapham, but was probably a released bird. Capercaillie were reintroduced to Scotland in 1837. This was successful but attempts in England in 1872-5 failed, as did an attempt in Cumbria in 1971. There are now around 1,000 birds in Scotland. This is only half the number present in 1992-4, which may indicate problems of habitat suitability.

Shrinking forests

When we talk of the extinct species of Britain what come to mind first are wolves, bears and other large predators. To a great extent these large mammals were associated with the woodlands that spread over much of the islands. The first, and largest, species to be lost was the brown bear.

The **brown bear** *Ursus arctos* was present in Britain until around a thousand years ago although it seems that it did not manage to recolonise Ireland after the Ice Ages. Bears were well established throughout Britain however, living in the extensive forests and feeding on the fruit, birds and small mammals (and occasionally deer) that lived there. At one time they would have been the most abundant large predators, with estimates of Stone Age populations of around 17,000 individuals. As such it was inevitable that bears would be in conflict with humans, both as a direct physical threat and as a killer of lambs. Bears have always been hunted by humans and as the human population increases, so bear populations around the world decline.

There are surprisingly few direct records of bears in Britain. There are some physical remains, but most are from Ice Age times. More recent remains include a bear pelt found in 2011 in a burial chamber on Dartmoor in Devon. This was dated to 4,000 years ago and probably represents a trophy made from a native bear. The most recent physical remains are a jaw in Colchester dated to the 11-14th century and one from Carlisle from the 12-13th centuries. These, and

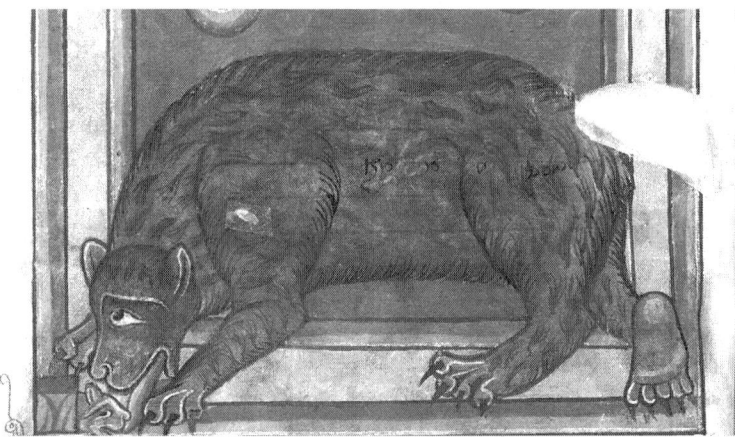

Brown bear: for some reason bears were thought to give birth to formless cubs, which they then licked into shape. From a bestiary from 1230-40 (British Library, Harley MS 4751)

15

claws found in York from Anglo-Saxon levels could be either relics of some of the last British bears or the remains of bears, or parts of bears, imported from Europe.

The Roman occupation of Britain provides us with a little more concrete information. Martial's 'Liber Spectaculorum' from 81AD mentions that bears were imported for the games in the newly opened Colosseum in Rome:

"...Laureolus ... offered his defenceless entrails to a Caledonian bear..."

It seems from this that bears were still to be found in Scotland at least. Much later, the Domesday Book for Norfolk records that each year the City of Norfolk sent a bear to King Edward for baiting.

"The whole of the borough paid £20 to the King TRE ['tempora regis Eduardis' - in the time of King Edward the Confessor, i.e. 1042-66] and £10 to the earl, along with 21s. 4d. to the prebendaries, six sextaires of honey, a bear, and six dogs for the bear."

There may not have been bears in Norfolk at this time, but Norwich must have been obtaining its bears from somewhere. They could have been importing them from Europe, or from Scotland. Sometime in the dark ages between the 1st and the 11th centuries the bear was lost as a British species. It is sometimes said that the brown bear was last recorded in England in the 8th century and in Scotland until the 10th century, but neither date has much reliability. All that is certain is that the brown bear was the both the first and the largest large British mammal to be lost in historical times.

Although it is clear that the woodland habitat that survives today is a pale shadow of its former greatness, the natural extent of woodland over Britain is a source of dispute among ecologists. Was it complete cover, or was Scotland only partly forested? Even in England, generally accepted to be naturally largely wooded, was there a great forest blanketing the country or a mosaic of woods and grassy areas? Whatever the answers, it is clear that there was vastly more forest that there is today, or was even in mediaeval times.

What woodland we do have is relatively young; there are ancient trees but they are old survivors in largely replanted, managed habitat. The forests are also quite uniform. There are the forestry monocultures of introduced spruce, good for very few animals, and there are the more diverse woods, but few British woods have anything like a natural composition of species or ages of trees.

A large number of the beetles that seem to have disappeared from Britain were associated with the ancient, diverse forests. One of the

The romantic view of the old British forests: 'An ancient beech tree' by P. Sandby 1794

first to go may have been the **blue stag beetle** *Platycerus caraboides* which was last recorded in 1839. There are just a few old records of this species and it has been suggested to be an introduction. The first records are very imprecise, possibly from Bristol. The most accurately recorded specimens were collected by the Rev. F.W. Hope whose collections formed the basis of the Hope Collection, the core of the Oxford University Zoology Museum's entomology collections. Hope was an undergraduate at Oxford in 1819-22 and collected many beetles in Wytham Woods just outside Oxford, including the blue stag beetle. The last record was 1839 from Windsor.

Windsor Forest was also the last known home of the **longhorn beetle** *Strangalia attenuata*. This had been recorded from Wiltshire, Berkshire and south Essex but vanished in around 1845. This species feeds on a variety of deciduous trees and probably become extinct as a result of the clearance of some forests in the 1800s, although there were also unconfirmed reports of this species from Hombush Forest, West Sussex in 1892.

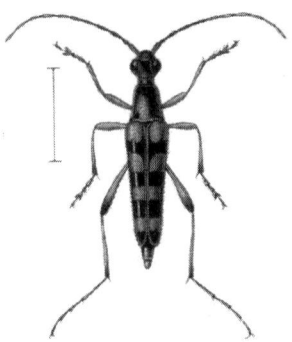

Strangalia attenuata longhorn beetle after Reitter 1908-17

Another enigmatic species lost at much the same time was the **false flower beetle** *Scraptia dubia*. This is known in Britain from a single specimen; a beetle collected in 1842 on a window in Glanville's Wootton, Dorset. Wootton Glanville, alternatively called Glanville's Wootton, is within the area of the ancient forest of Blackinore. This forest no longer exists and as the beetles feed on fungus in rotten wood, both as adults and larvae, the clearance of the forest probably caused the extinction of the population. We have no idea how many species were similarly affected but did not register their position by conveniently venturing into a house occupied by an entomologist at the right moment. These species will forever be missing from any list of the British fauna. One very clearly recorded case of extinction, but also mysterious is that of the 'Manchester moth'.

The **Manchester moth** *Euclemensia woodiella* is probably the most interesting extinction of the 1800s. This small yellow and brown moth was found by the amateur entomologist Robert Cribb in mid-June 1829. He found around 50 or 60 individuals in a rotting tree on Kersal Moor in Salford. He gave one to R. Wood and two to S. Carter. Wood asked the entomologist John Curtis to identify his specimen and Curtis named the species *Pancalia woodiella* after him, unfortunately overlooking the fact that Cribb was the collector. Cribb was so offended that he refused to have anything to do with other collectors or entomologists for some years. No-one else was able to locate the species and some collectors even accused Cribb of having passed off a foreign moth as British, even though Cribb's collection was exclusively British, further upsetting Cribb. Eventually Curtis persuaded him part with some more of the moths. In the meantime Cribb had pawned the box of moths to the landlady of a pub or lodging-house. When Cribb and Curtis came to select the moths they found the box had been thrown onto a fire and destroyed. As a result the three specimens given to Wood and Curtis are all that remains of the Manchester moth. Despite searches it has not been found in Britain, or anywhere else in Europe. There have been suggestions that the species was not native, as the other members of the genus, all North American, have larvae that parasitize kermes scale insects, the European species of which seem too small to support the Manchester moth. Even if this is true, it has also not been found in North America.

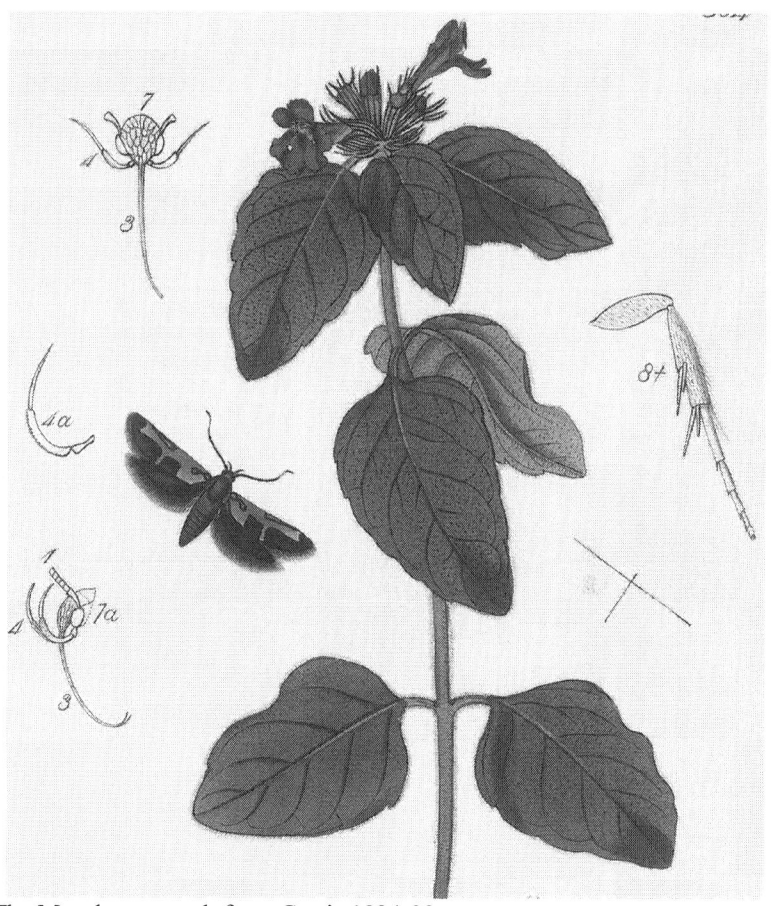

The Manchester moth from Curtis 1824-39

A major cause of extinction of woodland beetles has been the removal of dead wood, originally for firewood and later for disease control in forestry management. An enormous number of beetle species feed on dead wood, such as the **capuchin beetle** *Bostrichus capucinus*. Until 1908 this beetle could be found in north-west England but with the loss of most standing dead wood it has gone. The **cylindrical bark beetle** *Endophloeus markovichianus* was recorded only in the New Forest in 1862 and 1927. It lives under the bark of dead beech trees standing in the sun. It is thus highly vulnerable to clearance of dead wood.

Longhorn beetles also depend on trees for larval development. The **reddish longhorn beetle** *Obrium cantharinum* was found in the south-east of England in the 19th century. It was mainly recorded from Hertfordshire and Essex. In the 20th century there are records from Kent, and the last record is from Bovey Tracey in south Devon in 1929. In Europe these beetles are associated with deciduous forests, the larvae living in dead wood of deciduous trees,

Reddish longhorn beetle from Curtis 1924-39

especially the white polar and aspen, while the adults feed on flowers. It is likely to have disappeared due to changes in land use resulting in loss of standing dead wood.

Most moths are much more dependent on the growing plants in the forests than on the wood of the trees themselves. The **speckled beauty moth** *Faginovora arenaria* was a British species until 1898. It is still found in Europe but is in decline everywhere due to loss of the oak woodlands with which it is associated, depending on old trees for the lichens on which its larvae feed.

The **gypsy moth** *Lymantria dispar* would seem to be a surprising casualty. This is a notorious invasive species in North America, but is native to Eurasia. Its larvae feed on the leaves of deciduous trees and as great numbers of eggs are laid they can defoliate much of the tree. The caterpillars are hairy and their hairs can be skin irritants, inducing allergic reactions in some people. It was resident in Britain until around 1910, with a last record in 1907. It declined with the reduction of woodlands and survived last in the small woods in the fens. The conversion of those areas into agriculture in the early to mid-20th century probably led to the loss of the last colonies. Fortunately this was only a temporary extinction and recently it has recolonised the islands with populations located since 1995 in London and since 2005 in Buckinghamshire, Dorset and the Channel Islands. Females are poor flyers, or flightless and how the moths recolonised is not known; larvae may have been accidentally introduced on vehicles from mainland Europe.

The **flame brocade moth** *Trigonophora flammea* was present in Sussex until 1919. The only surviving British population is in the Channel Islands. Adults flying from Europe have appeared, usually at coastal light-traps along England's southern shores, mainly from Hampshire westwards. The normal flight period is October and November, and most immigrants arrive in November. The caterpillar feeds on low plants such as buttercup in the early stages, later preferring such species as ash and privet which suggests that the moth could re-establish itself in the future. The **union rustic moth** *Apamea* (or *Eremobina*) *pabulatricula* was present in isolated colonies in central Scotland (Clyde and Tay) down to East Anglia. The main populations were in Yorkshire and Lincolnshire. These declined and in 1919 they were last recorded in Lincolnshire and in 1936 in Hertfordshire. The few subsequent records are probably migrants. The native populations were lost with the clearance of woodlands in the 19th and early 20th centuries as the adults tend to roost on the trunks of oak trees, while the larvae feed on grasses, especially the purple moor-grass. This means that the moth requires a mosaic of deciduous woodland and marshy ground, conditions which were found in the floodplains that were drained in the early 20th century.

The **dusky clearwing moth** *Paranthrene tabaniformis* was never commonly recorded in Britain but has not been seen since 1924. The larvae feed under the bark of poplars (mainly aspen), willow and sea-buckthorn trees, which remain abundant. However, the dusky clearwing was recorded from woodland trees in Epping Forest (1839), Hampshire (1909) and finally from Berkshire. It probably requires healthy woodlands containing the host plants, rather than the isolated trees that remain, or have been planted, since the clearance of the southern English woodlands in the 19th and 20th centuries.

The **conformist moth** *Lithophane furcifera* was present in small numbers in Glamorgan, Wales until 1959. This population was a British subspecies, the dark form *suffusa*. A paler European form *furcifera* was occasionally recorded in England until 1946. It was seen again in Northumberland in 2007 and in Scotland in 2011. The larvae feed on the leaves of various trees, including elm, oak, willow and poplar. In contrast to this varied range of host plants, the **cudweed moth** *Cucullia gnaphalii* feeds on leaves and flowers of goldenrod growing in ancient woodland. Goldenrod is still fairly abundant but declining. It is the combination of the declining food plant and the loss of the woodland that led to the extinction of the populations of Hampshire, Surrey and Essex. The last record was in Oxfordshire in 1979.

The **orange upperwing moth** *Jodia croceago* occurred in small populations in southern England and Wales where the larvae fed on oak. It was restricted to Cornwall, Devon, Sussex, Surrey, Shropshire and South Wales by 1980 and continued to decline, surviving only in Sussex in 1983. It has not been seen since except for one found in Sussex in 2006 but this is thought to be a vagrant from Europe. It is associated with the open woodland and woodland

Conformist moth from South 1907

edges, especially coppiced woods. The decline of the species is probably associated with changed woodland management, especially the decline in coppicing which has resulted in denser woodland, not suited to this species.

It is not just the moths that are dependant on very specific food plants. The **juniper bug** *Chlorochroa juniperina* was mainly a southern European species and southern Britain was on the northern limits of its range until its extinction in 1925. It was highly vulnerable to changes in the abundance of its sole host-plant – juniper. Through the extensive clearance and change of woodlands in southern Britain juniper declined, becoming largely restricted to Scotland. Juniper is now widely planted as an ornamental, but the juniper bug has disappeared.

Even animals that do not feed on any of the woodland plants may be closely tied to the habitat. The **two-tubercled orbweb spider** *Gibbaranea bituberculata* was recorded only in Burnham Beeches in Buckinghamshire in 1908, with a questionable report from Essex in the 1940s. It lives in open woodland where it spins its webs in bushes in the open. The vegetation of the Burnham Beeches site was completely cleared in 1954 and the species has not been seen since.

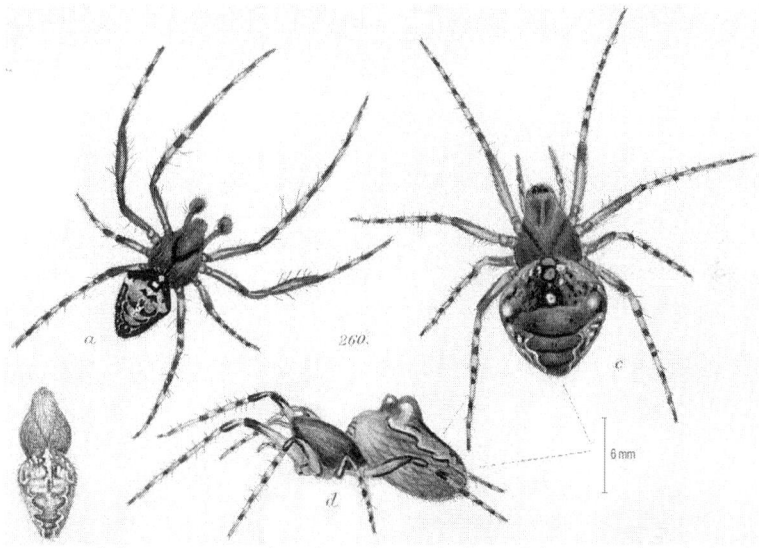

Gibbaranea globosa, a more abundant close relative of the two-tubercled spider, from Blackwall 1864

Britain was not completely deforested, and the loss of woodlands halted in the late 20th century. Since then forestry land, private woodlands and community forests have increased in extent, encouraging the return of some woodland species. The majority of these will be inconspicuous invertebrates like the species described above, but there is one exception. **Wild boar** *Sus scrofa* were found wherever there was forest in Britain until the middle ages and were probably the most abundant large mammal after the red deer until around 1200. Although once common throughout England, Wales and Scotland, there are no clear records from Ireland, and the bones and accounts of ferocious wild pigs there seem to be feral domestic pigs rather than genuinely wild boar.

Boar were a source of food from the first arrival of humans in the islands and became one of the most prized of game animals. By the 11th century they had become a royal prerogative and in 1087 William I's laws of the forest decreed that anyone killing a deer or boar was to be punished by losing their eyes. The last boar of Durham was reportedly killed by Roger de Ferry in 1200. Boar could still be found in large numbers in some areas and a feast for Henry III in 1251 included 300 boar from the Forests of Dean and Pickering. In 1260 the King obtained just 12 from the Forest of Dean and they are not mentioned from there for the next 740 years. 1260 seems to be the last record of a genuine wild boar in England. They lived on in Scotland, although there too they were in decline. In 1263 the Sheriff of Forfar's accounts included the cost of corn to support the wild boars, a provision that would have been unimaginable two hundred years earlier.

There are some late stories of wild boar, such as the giant boar killed near St. Andrews in 1520. In 1541 wild boar were either extinct in Scotland or nearly so, for in that year in order to have boar on his estate at Falkland King James V had to import three from France. These imports from France had started earlier (13th century) in England and are the likely source of wild boar kept at Chartley Park, Staffordshire in 1573.

Attempts to re-establish wild boar in the wild were made in the 18th and 19th centuries in hunting estates. King James I released animals from France and later from Germany into Windsor Park in 1608 and 1611. Charles I released boar into the New Forest from Germany. They did not become established and had died out by the end of the 17th century. In the 1980s farmed wild boar started escaping, especially in 1987 when a hurricane across southern England brought down many trees, damaging enclosures and enabling many boar to escape. Wild boar are now widespread. In 1998 the British government officially confirmed that the species was established and breeding on the Kent/East Sussex border (around 200-300) and in Dorset (fewer than 50). Breeding has since been

Wild boar from Johnstonus 1678

confirmed from the Forest of Dean. In 2006 the first wild boar for 400 years was seen in Scotland, near Fort William.

The most recent loss of a large animal in British woodlands was the **northern goshawk** *Accipipter gentilis*. This medium-sized forest hawk was never recorded in great numbers but was an established breeding species. The last records were from Lincolnshire in 1864 and Yorkshire in 1893. In both cases the nests were destroyed and the female shot. This sums up the threats they faced: persecution as predators.

Although breeding stopped in the late 19th century goshawks still visited from the European population. There were several breeding attempts between 1921 and 1951 but all the birds involved were killed. At the same time birds were being imported for falconry and some of these escaped or were released deliberately. These, combined with other European arrivals, formed a small breeding population from 1970.

Draining the swamp

Man has changed the British landscape since Stone Age times and no part of the British isles can be said to be natural today. Of all the habitats of the islands the one most altered is swamp-land. The meres and fens have been exploited for their rich animal life and drained for more than 1000 years to make use of the rich marsh muds for agricultural land.

The earliest known losses came as a result of hunting. **Common cranes** *Grus grus* have never been common British birds (despite their name). They were regular migrants, but possibly only irregular breeders in the islands. Hunting for sport put an end to even occasional breeding. In Britain the last breeding was in 1542, and around 1800 in Ireland.

Cranes live around ponds in forests, moorlands, bogs and marshes. All these habitats were very extensively modified through the 18th, 19th and early 20th centuries, but from the 1950s small numbers of cranes have been regular visitors. In 1979 four birds arrived in the Norfolk Broads. Two stayed and bred in 1981. Breeding has occurred every year since then but the population has only grown very slowly. Yorkshire has had a breeding pair since 2002 and East Anglia (three

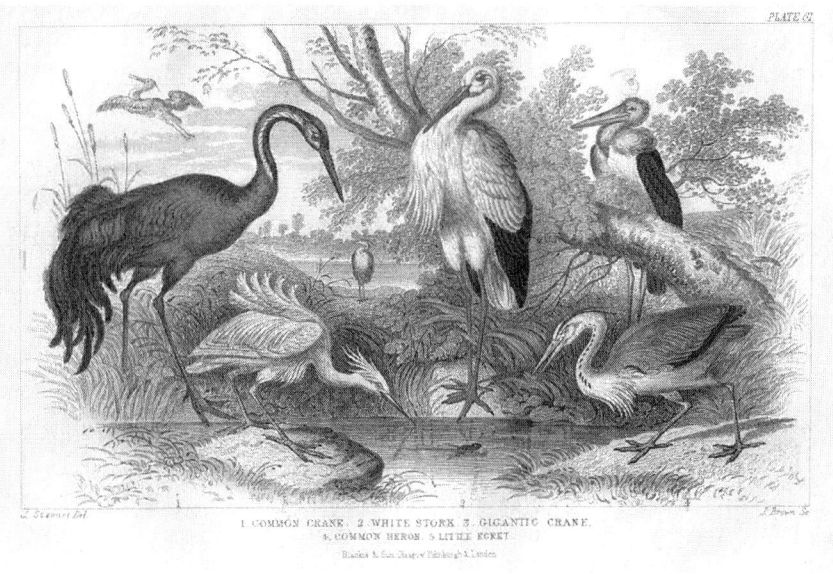

Common crane (on left) from Goldsmith 1865

pairs) since 2007. In 2010 there was a total of 13-14 breeding pairs, with a wintering population of about 50 birds. Some birds were moved to Somerset to re-establish a breeding population there. Cranes have also started visiting Ireland once again, with 30 arriving in county Cork in 2011.

Eurasian spoonbills *Platalea leucorodia* are also breeding in Norfolk after a long absence. However, there have only ever been three isolated breeding records so it seems not to have been an established British species until recently.

Other wetland birds that have disappeared and then recolonised include the **black-tailed godwit** *Limosa limosa*. This stopped breeding in Yorkshire and East Anglia in 1829, in Cambridgeshire in 1847, Norfolk in 1857 and finally Lincolnshire in 1885. This decline seems to have been due to fenland drainage and shooting. In 1937 breeding attempts took place in Lincolnshire and since 1961 they have bred in Cambridgeshire and Norfolk. **Ruff** *Philomachus pugnax* were also notable breeders in the 16th century but declined and are now erratic breeders.

These last few bird species have declined at least in part as a result of habitat loss from drainage. It was not until the 19th century that drainage was carried out on a significant scale, particularly from the 1820 when wind-powered pumps were replaced with steam drainage pumps. The agricultural and industrial revolutions added siltation and pollution to the toxic mix of threats. Electric pump hastened the drainage following World War II and today only 10% remains of the area of the area of fens that were still present in 1934. Not surprisingly extinction was early and extensive in the wetlands, starting with a particularly conspicuous example arising from drainage.

The **large copper** *Lycena dispar* is a conspicuous butterfly that was first recorded from Dozen's Bank near Spalding in Lincolnshire in 1749. It was last seen in the British Isles in 1851 at Bottisham in Cambridgeshire. This species was lost in Britain due to draining of the fens. In Europe it has a patchy distribution but may be common in isolated colonies. Several attempts have been made to reintroduce the species. The British population was an endemic subspecies *L. d. dispar*, now extinct so reintroduced butterflies have been of the Netherlands subspecies *L. d. batavus*. The first release took place in 1927 at Woodwalton Fen, in Huntingdonshire. This established a viable population which survived until an exceptional flood in 1968 submerged the larval food plants (great water dock). In 1969 only one male and four females emerged but failed to breed. Some individuals had been maintained in captivity and further releases took place in 1970 (1068 butterflies), 1971 (552), 1972 (724) and 1973 (1000). None of these succeeded and the species is once again extinct in Britain.

Large copper from Curtis 1824-39

Fenland drainage was also responsible for the loss of fen associated moths in the 1880s. The **many-lined moth** *Costaconvexa polygrammata* was found in the East Anglian fens until 1875. There have been more recent records from the south coast, which are of vagrant individuals from Europe where it is widespread. The reed and sedge eating **reed tussock moth** *Laelia coenosa* was recorded from the fens in Cambridgeshire and Huntingdonshire until 1879. Collecting may have contributed to the loss of this species although the main cause was probably the loss of many reed-beds.

The **weevil** *Bagous binodulus* may have been lost for the same reason. The surviving populations in northern and central Europe feed on water soldiers which remain abundant. However, drainage of wetlands may have led to extinction of its naturally isolated populations. It was reportedly "found occasionally in Battersea-fields, and also in the marshes near Norwich." It was last recorded in 1861.

The drainage of the great marshes, the meres and fens of East Anglia, Lincolnshire and Cambridgeshire resulted in the loss of important habitats and the consequent loss of some **diving beetles**. *Rhantus aberratus* was plentiful near Cambridge and many were collected there by Charles Darwin in 1829, but has not been seen since 1904. This year was also the last time the **water beetle** *Hydroporus aberrans* was found in the last remnant of Whittlesea Mere in Cambridgeshire. **Chequered history beetles** *Graphoderus bilineatus* were only ever recorded in Britain from near Catfield Fen in east Norfolk between 1905 and 1910. This species became extinct due to habitat changes due to pollution as nutrients running off farmland accumulated in the remaining pools.

An early fenland species loss was the **fen spider** *Hypsosinga heri* known from Wicken Fen in Cambridgeshire in 1892 and 1912. There are also old, imprecise records from Berkshire. The species is found on plants near water and lowering of the water table at Wicken Fen during the extensive fen drainage in the early 20th century may have made the site unsuitable by turning boggy ground into dry land.

The **orache moth** *Trachea atriplicis* was formerly resident in the East Anglian and Cambridgeshire fens, it also declined in the fen drainage and was last recorded in these areas in 1915. A number of records since refer to migrants, mainly on the south and east coasts in July and August. The species remains fairly common in much of continental Europe, where the larvae feed on orache and goosefoot, amongst a range of other low plants.

Not all species vanished abruptly; the filter feeding **water beetle** *Sphercheus emarginatus* was originally found in fenland from the east of

England to mid-west Yorkshire. It survived longer than many fenland species and was last recorded in 1956 from Beccles, East Suffolk.

Although the most obvious losses were in the great marshes of the east of Britain, wetland loss has also occurred at a smaller scale within other habitats. One of the most severely affected groups of animals has been the water beetles both in large and small wetlands. These depend upon very specific types of water-bodies: some species require large ponds, others small, temporary pools. All are vulnerable to drainage and pollution. The **water beetle** *Ochthebius aeneus* was found in exposed ponds with little vegetation on the Surrey heaths. Most of the heathlands were forest in prehistoric times and developed their characteristics after forest clearance. If not maintained they are invaded by shrubs and would eventually return to forest. In order to preserve the rare animals and plants that depend on them, heaths need to be maintained. Clearing of heathland for housing development and neglect has led to 85% of the area of heathland in Surrey being lost in the past 200 years. The beetle was last recorded from 'St. Leonards' in 1913. It is not clear exactly where this is; it was thought to be at Hastings but is probably St. Leonard's Fleet, Winchelsea.

A Suffolk dike in the 1880s, photo from Emerson 1887

Similarly the **diving beetle** *Rhantus bistriatus* was found in temporary ponds in open land, at Potter Heigham, Norfolk, in Essex, Norfolk, Cambridgeshire and Huntingdonshire. It was probably lost after its last sighting in 1913 because of fenland drainage.

Some wetland habitats are highly specialised, and peat bogs are some of the most fragile of all. The **whirligig beetle** *Gyrinus natator* beetle was formerly found in Westmorland and Cumberland in Newton Reigny Moss and Cliburn Moss until 1902. These areas were cut for peat, and the Newton Reigny Moss also became polluted.

Although drainage was an early problem in wetlands, it was not the only issue. In the 20th century pollution became a major cause of extinction. Caddis flies are highly sensitive to water pollution and today many species are used as indicators of the health of rivers. Almost all are found around streams as adults, and the larvae live in the water, requiring clean, well oxygenated water. As a result they have declined wherever waters have been polluted. Throughout the 19th and 20th centuries many species declined, although only one species has been known to be extinct in Britain. The **caddis fly** *Hydropsyche exocellata* was present in the Thames, from Weybridge and Kent to Richmond. It was first recorded in 1865 but has not been found since 1901. Another species of caddisfly was thought to be extinct but has been rediscovered. The **pincer-tailed caddisfly** *Hydroptila tigurina* was recorded at Ambleside in Cumbria in 1881 and not located again until 2010 when it was found in Assynt in Scotland.

The **mayfly** *Arthroplea congener* is one of the species that is difficult to evaluate; it is a European species known from Britain by a single specimen collected at Stanmore, Middlesex in 1920. This could be a naturally very rare species on the edge of its range or simply a vagrant individual. Mayflies have famously short lives and this makes vagrants and natural colonisation of islands extremely unlikely. However, there are mayflies on oceanic islands so it is not completely impossible. If this species was resident in Britain and is now extinct it is likely to have been the result of the pollution of the British rivers in the early 20th century.

This pollution was probably the cause of the extinction of a fish, the **houting** *Coregonus oxyrinchus*, in around 1900. This freshwater fish was found in the rivers draining into the North Sea in England, France, Belgium, the Netherlands and Germany. None of these populations survive. A Danish population does survive but may be a different species. The last of the western populations died in 1940 (Germany). In Britain it was recorded from Lincolnshire (1877), Chichester (1880) and the mouth of the River Medway

(1881). It was never recorded in marine waters, only in fresh or brackish estuaries, and the British fish were probably a rare ancient relict population, finally drive to extinction by the concentration of pollutants in these rivers.

By the middle of the 20th century British waterways were in a terrible state and this general poor health may have caused the extinction of the **dainty damselfly** *Coenagrion scitulum*. This was the first British damselfly to be lost, unusually for a wetland animal when flooding destroyed its breeding sites. On 31st January 1953 a storm combined with a high spring tide resulted in a dramatic flood across the Netherlands, Belgium and eastern England and Scotland. The Netherlands were worst affected, with 1,836 people killed. In Britain the impact was much less, with 307 deaths in England and 19 in Scotland. It was the impact of this storm that led to the construction of the Thames Barrier. Ecologically the impacts were severe as sea-water flooded over large areas of flat land, including marshland, resulting in a failed breeding year for many freshwater associated species. Floods on this scale are rare events but the decline in wetland areas and quality must have made the dainty damselfly species more vulnerable to extinction; had the wetlands been in a better state the species would probably have survived. A Channel Islands population of the damselfly did survive on Guernsey until 1956 but by then there was no longer sufficient wetland habitat on the island to support it. In 2010 the dainty damselfly reappeared in Kent as individuals apparently blown over the English Channel. It may re-establish itself in the future.

The **Norfolk damselfly** *Coenagrion armatum* was first recorded in Britain from Sutton, Stalham and Hickling Broads within the Norfolk Broads in 1903 but was last seen in 1956. It disappeared due to the open water in the broads changing to dry reedbed. It depends on the open water as its eggs are laid in the stems of the aquatic plants that stand in the water. In this case the changed waterways became clogged with silt from the surrounding agricultural land.

In contrast the **orange-spotted emerald dragonfly** *Oxygastra curtisii* was found in slow flowing streams and ponds in southern England and was probably lost to pollution. There were only two known localities: the River Stour and the Moors River in Devon (1820 to 1963) and the River Tamar in Devon (1946).

The two most recently recorded marshland extinctions probably succumbed to simple loss of habitat. In 1986 the **Pashford pot beetle** *Cryptocephalus exiguus* disappeared from Pashford Poors Fen in Suffolk. This tiny (2mm) beetle was found in the Norfolk Broads and Lincolnshire Fens in the 19th century. By 1910 it was restricted to Pashford Poors Fen; it disappeared from there as well in 1957. It was rediscovered in 1980 but 6 years later was lost once again. The larvae live in small clay pots (hence the common name) which they construct in damp ground and so are dependent on the wetland habitat. The reduction in area of the habitat simply meant that the population was reduced to a point where it was no longer viable.

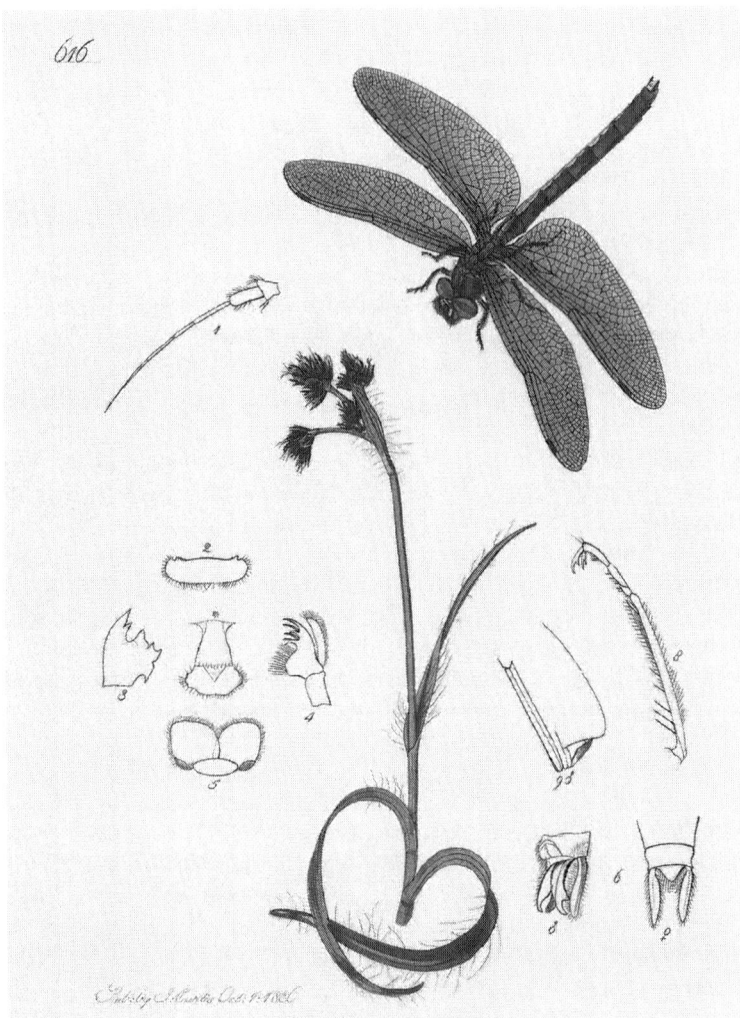

Orange-spotted emerald dragonfly, from Curtis 1824-39

At only 2mm it is possible that the Pashford pot beetle does survive somewhere, overlooked. The same cannot be said for the much more conspicuous **pool frog** *Rana lessonae* which died out two years before the beetle disappeared. Several frog species survived in Britain until around 1,000 years ago but declined or disappeared following ancient climate changes. These are known from bones found in Lincolnshire (dated to 880-1040AD) and identified as the pool frog, moor frog *Rana arvalis* (otherwise known only before 1,000BC), the agile frog *R.* cf. *dalmatia* (also known from 1,000BC, but still present on the Channel Islands). Of these, only the pool frog survived into historical times with a relict population in the east of England until the end of the 20th century. As the wetlands shrank the frogs retreated, disappearing from the wild in 1995 and the last native pool frog is thought to have been the one that died in captivity in 1999 at Thompson Common, Norfolk. Today there are pool frogs in the east of England but these are thought to be descended from introduced animals, or are from a recent reintroduction to Norfolk (from 2005).

Many wetland species are good dispersers, able to fly long distances between patches of ephemeral habitat. These may be able to recolonise wetlands whenever they are in a suitable condition. For example, the **black tern** *Chlidonias niger* does not seem to have been widely distributed in Britain but apparently bred in large numbers in the east of England, from Yorkshire to Kent,

A pot beetle, related to the Pashford pot beetle. From Curtis 1824-39

in the 18th century. It breeds and feeds in marshes and drainage of these habitats was probably the cause of extinction. As the marshes were drained most breeding populations disappeared, although they did return temporarily in some areas when sites became flooded. They do not seem to have been hunted deliberately although there was some egg collecting in the 1840s. They had disappeared from Yorkshire and Lincolnshire by the 1850s. In Cambridgeshire there is only one breeding record, from Bottisham in 1824, a particularly good year for the species. 1858 was the last recorded breeding in Norfolk, and 1860 the last for Oxfordshire. There were unconfirmed records from Essex, Suffolk and Cumberland. Romney Marsh was the last stronghold of the species in Britain, with large numbers there until the 1840s. It declined throughout the second half of the 19th century and only 5-6 pairs remained by 1884.

Although black terns were sighted as non-breeding visitors there was a long gap in breeding, with no records from 1884 until eight pairs bred in 1941 in the Pett Level of Sussex. This was the result of an unusual event; the deliberate flooding in 1940 of the area as part of the coastal defences against possible German invasion during the Second World War. The accuracy of this record has been questioned. A definite breeding did take place in 1967 a year after the Ouse Washes flooded. A breeding attempt in the same place in 1975 failed, as did an attempt in Nottinghamshire in the same year, this time due to an egg collector.

Black tern from Morris 1850-7

Similarly erratic breeding seems to have been normal for the obscure **Baillon's crake** *Porzana pusilla*. This small water bird was recorded as a breeding species throughout England in the 19th century. The first record was from the River Waveney in Suffolk in 1819 and it bred on at least four occasions: in Cambridgeshire in 1858, Dorset in 1882, Norfolk in 1866 and 1889. It bred in sedge beds which were mostly lost through fenland drainage. It declined throughout western Europe but has recovered in northern Europe recently and there have been increasing numbers of records of sightings of visiting Baillon's crakes throughout Britain. Breeding has been suspected in the past few years but not confirmed. In 2012 one was seen in Ireland for the first time in 160 years.

Although many wetland species have been lost, their extinction has probably not affected the ecosystems in any significant way, certainly when compared to the changes that caused their extinction in the first place. The loss of one species though has changed the wetland environment. This species was lost even before marsh drainage started on any significant scale. **European beavers** *Castor fiber* do not modify the landscape on anything like the scale of its American relative: their dams are smaller as are the animals themselves. Even so, their activity turns straight, fast flowing rivers into slower, meandering streams and pools which benefits flood management and most aquatic animals. In addition their grazing alters riverside vegetation through coppicing of stream-side trees and shrubs. Since their loss the British riverside must have changed dramatically.

Beavers were present in Britain from the end of the Ice Ages. They do not cross sea waters and although they were able to colonise mainland Britain when it was connected to Europe by low sea-levels, Ireland and the islands remained isolated and so were not colonised. Their disappearance from Britain was not as an accident of habitat change but resulted from being directly hunted to extinction.

They were regarded as one of the most precious fur-bearing animals and were hunted extensively. In Wales the 940 AD Laws of Howel the Good valued a beaver pelt at 120 pence, compared to just 24 pence for a marten or 12 for an otter. They became extinct in England in Saxon times, in Wales at the end of the 12th century and Scotland in the 16th century.

Beavers seem still to have been abundant in Scotland in the early 12th century based on records of furs collected. They were still hunted in large numbers in the mid 12th century as indicated by records of duties paid on pelts. By 1188 they were restricted to the River Teifi in Cardiganshire according to the writings of Sylvester Giraldus de Barri, but as he never visited Scotland this may be questionable. There is a mention of rare beaver pelts in Ayr around 1320, during the reign of Robert the Bruce, but these may have been imported rather than Scottish beavers. As late as 1526 beavers are included in a list of animals present around Loch Ness but it is notable that a 1424 list of duties paid on furs does not include beaver, suggesting that commercial trapping had failed long before. It seems probable that extinction occurred around 1200.

In May 2009 eleven Norwegian beavers were released to Knapdale Forest, Argyll, Scotland as a trial reintroduction. A further five were released the following year. This was planned as a five-year experiment to provide information on the impacts of a reintroduction. The experiment was judged to have been highly successful, paving the way for a full reintroduction in the future. Although this is a reintroduction trial there are already beavers established in Scotland. Somewhere between 120 and 150 live in the River Tay. These are the fifth generation descendants of beavers that escaped from captivity. They were first noticed in 2007, with a possible earlier sighting in 2001. There is also a small population of beavers, again escaped from captivity, in Devon. The future of this latter group is currently uncertain as the British government has declared an intention to eradicate them as they had not been released as part of a planned reintroduction. Whether they will be removed in the face of opposition remains to be seen.

Beaver from Philippe de Thaon's translation of Bestiarius, made in England in around 1300 – clearly beavers were already too scarce for the artist ever to have seen one

Dig for victory

Following the first clearance of the great British forests in prehistoric times the agricultural revolution was the event that changed the landscape most rapidly and dramatically. In the 18th century changes in land use altered everything, creating the countryside we know today. This landscape has been in continual change since then, with changes in field size, planting and then removal of hedgerows, changes in crops and grazing practices, and particularly since the World Wars, mechanisation and the introduction of artificial fertilisers and insecticides.

One of the most fragile of the agricultural habitats is chalk grassland. This is geographically restricted, depending on the underlying chalk geology for its existence in the first place. It also depends on grazing, being an artificial habitat, at least in a large and stable form. In the absence of grazing animals it becomes invaded by scrub and trees. Sheep and rabbits keep it the way we tend to think it should be. Where we have reduced grazing pressure the scrub takes over and when myxomatosis was introduced to control the rabbit population in 1953 the grasslands changed rapidly. Where the scrub took over, chalk grassland specialists disappeared.

An early loss was the **leaf beetle** *Cryptocephalus violaceus* which was recorded only from chalk slopes on the Kent coast and in Cambridgeshire until 1864. This was followed by other beetles with similar ranges: the **weevil** *Ceutorhynchus hepaticus* found in chalk grassland in Sussex and the **weevil** *Tychius polylineatus* in Cambridgeshire, Berkshire and Sussex. Both were last seen in 1909.

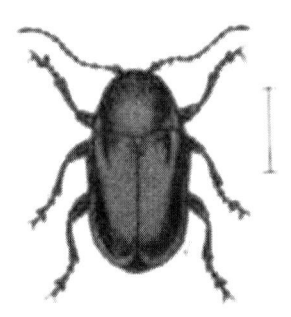

Leaf beetle *Cryptocephalus violaceus* from Calwer & Jager 1876

Although these beetles were the first recorded losses, they were soon followed by other insects. **Cullum's bumblebee** *Bombus cullumanus* was first identified in Suffolk and named after a local naturalist Sir Thomas Cullum. It was found in the south-east of England but was always rare. In the 1920s it could still be found in the Seaford area of Sussex and was last recorded in 1941 in Berkshire. It is also declining in Europe and is threatened throughout its range. It is associated with chalk grassland and has probably declined because of changes in agricultural practices.

The **Lewes wave moth** *Scopula immorata* was found in only one site in Britain, in a woodland at Lewes in East Sussex. It was last recorded there in 1961. This tiny population would have been extremely vulnerable to any deterioration of its habitat. Although it was recorded from a woodland it is normally associated with dry grassland, so was probably dependant on the chalk grasslands around the site. The **feathered ear moth** *Pachetra sagittigera* used to be found in the chalk downs of southern England, such as in Portland, Devon, where the larvae fed on grasses. It was described as a British subspecies: *brittanica*, which differed from the European form in being paler. It was last seen in 1963.

Sandy fields are also a particularly sensitive agricultural habitat. In 1902 the only known records were made of two beetle species: *Hypocoprus latridioides* from under cow pats on a sandy field at Brandon, Suffolk and *Philonthus confinis* from Kent and Worcestershire (the latter known only from three records). The **weevil** *Lixus vilis* was known from the south coast sand dunes (e.g. Sandwich, Kent) until 1905. Its larvae live in the stems of common stork's bill which is a widespread but only locally common plant. In the same area the **oil beetle** *Meloe cicatricosus* was common from the 1840s, but was not recorded after 1906. Changes in land management saw the loss of the last population at Margate. *M. variegatus* showed a similar pattern of decline for the same reasons. This was apparently locally common in the 1800s when it was "taken by Mr Crow of Eversham, and since by Mr Milne near Margate in great plenty" but was last seen in 1882.

Meloe are known as "oil beetles" because they release oily droplets of haemolymph (insect blood) from their joints when disturbed; this contains a chemical, cantharidin, which causes blistering of the skin and painful swelling. The adults feed on pollen of common flowers such as dandelions, while the larvae are parasites of bees. As these beetles' larvae feed on the food stored by a single species or genus of bee, they are totally dependent on the survival of their host species. This close relationship to bees and the flightlessness of the adults makes them highly vulnerable to habitat change.

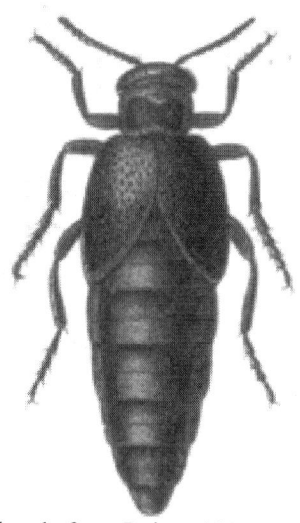

Meloe variegatus oil beetle from Reitter 1911

In *M. cicatricosus* the host is the potter flower bee *Anthophora retusa*. This bee was found throughout southern England until the middle of the 20th century but has declined, especially in the past 20 years, possibly due to agricultural intensification. It is now restricted to the south coast and is no longer found in Kent. It seems likely that habitat changes caused the decline of the bee, leading it turn to the loss of the beetle.

Another species, *M. mediterraneus* was more fortunate. This species was found in grassland in the south of England, from Kent, Essex and Devon. As with the other species, it seemed to have disappeared in around 1906 following changes in land management. However, it was rediscovered in 2012 by an oil beetle conservation project by the insect conservation organisation Buglife at Bolt Head in South Devon. There has been no sign of the other two species.

Other agricultural changes have seen meadows or fallow ground converted into more intensive arable land or 'improved' grazing land. The **chequer beetle** *Tilloidea unifasciatus* was recorded from several areas in south-east England. It was listed as being "on palings" in Hertfordshire occasionally and in Winsor according to Stephens in 1839 but was last recorded from Upper Norwood (Surrey) in 1877. It is associated with flowers and the reduction in weeds in agricultural land probably caused its loss.

An odd apparent extinction is one of the **glow-worm** species. *Lamprohiza splendidula* is in Britain only from two males collected in Kent in 1884. It is assumed that they had been abundant in the past but declined due to changes in agriculture, although it is not known if they were fully established in Britain.

More clear-cut examples are two **weevils** that disappeared from Britain in the same year. *Bagous diglyptus* was first recorded in Britain in 1879 near Burton-on-Trent, and subsequently from Derby, Suffolk and Norfolk. The last definite record was from 1897 near the River Gipping at Ipswich; records from the Norfolk Broads in 1906 and 1913 were misidentifications. It is associated with the meadow saxifrage which has a scattered distribution across Britain, growing on lime-rich lightly grazed grassland. The loss of the beetle may be a result of changes in grazing practices which caused a decline in the saxifrage. *Rhyncolus* (or *Phloeophagus*) *gracilis* was recorded from Sherwood forest. It probably declined due to land use changes, although its food plant, the beech, remains common.

'Improvement' of grazing land led to the loss of **Blunt's flat-body** or **purple carrot-seed moth** *Depressaria depressana* before 1900. This is a widespread moth found in Africa, Asia and Europe. In Britain it used to occur in the south-east of England (Surrey, Hampshire, Essex, Kent) but has not been found since the end of the 19th century. The larvae feed on common grassland plants such as wild carrot and wild parsnip. It may have declined as grasslands were managed and intensively grazed from the early 19th century. Adults have a very long over-wintering period, from September until May and changes in the unstable British climate may have contributed to its disappearance.

Carrot seed moth from Curtis 1924-39

A strange example is the **grass spider** *Mastigusa arietina*. This small spider was recorded from scattered localities in Surrey (Oxshott, Weybridge and Woking) and Berkshire (Windsor Forest and Wellington College). There is also an isolated record of a single female from Carlisle. This is an odd species it that it is found only in the nests of the ants *Lasius fuliginosus* and *L. brunneus* which are mainly found in oak stumps and dead trees in open country. It was only recorded between 1892 and 1926, although it was apparently not uncommon then. Removal of dead wood from farmland may have contributed to its rarity and apparent decline.

Simple expansion of the area of agriculture and its mechanisation resulted in the loss of many species between the World Wars. Several species of **mining bees** were lost in the 1930s and 1940s: *Halictus maculatus* and *Andrena nana* in 1930, *Andrena polita* in 1934, *Andrena floricola* in 1939, *Eucera tuberculata* in 1941, *Andrena tridentata* in 1944 and *Andrena vaga* in 1946. These bees made their nests in sandy ground with sparse vegetation. The **marsh dagger moth** *Acronicta strigosa* was present in the Midlands and south-east England. Since 1933 there has been only a single record, a migrant individual in East Sussex in 1996. It is associated with mature hawthorn scrub and feeds on hawthorn and blackthorn. These were cleared in the agricultural intensification of the 19th and 20th centuries and this probably caused the extinction of the British population. This may also have caused the extinction of another hawthorn and blackthorn associate, the **blackthorn webworm moth** *Dichomeris derasella*. This is a central and eastern European species formerly found in Surrey (last seen in 1939).

An *Andrena* mining bee from Curtis 1924-39

The **minute seed moth** *Borkhausenia minutella* is an interesting case as its larvae feed on dead plant matter and seeds and it is mainly found around farm buildings. Improved seed storage and changes in farm building construction may be causing its decline across Europe. It may be regarded as a species that benefitted from old agricultural practices. It seems to have been common in Britain but disappeared after 1950.

There was a further dramatic intensification in British agriculture during and after the end of the Second World War. The area of cultivation had increased over the previous two centuries, but in the mid-late 20th century new practices were adopted, with increased mechanisation, and the application of fertilisers and pesticides. This caused a dramatic change in the ecology of the countryside and many species declined. The decline of many farmland bird species has received much attention in recent years, but much less has been said about the disappearance of many insects. There are several likely victims of these changes, including the **great yellow bumblebee** *Bombus distinguendus* which was last seen in 1981.

For some of these species we can be very specific as to why the changes in the countryside have caused their extinction. The **leaf beetle** *Chrysomela tremula* was last recorded in 1958. Along with many other species it depended on the specific characteristics of coppiced woodland. This management practice kept woods open, with high levels of light penetration resulting in abundant vegetation near the ground. Coppicing was almost completely abandoned in the

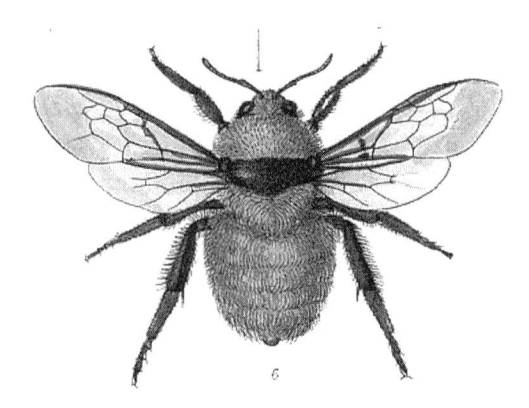

Great yellow bumblebee from Saunders 1896

20th century and the species associated with that management have declined. More recently it has been reintroduced as a management technique for conservation purposes, rather than for commercial reasons. Unfortunately for this particular beetle, the return of coppicing was too late.

Extinctions of species associated with agricultural habitats continued throughout the 20th century. The **spotted sulphur moth** *Emmelia trabealis* was only recorded as a resident species from Breckland in East Anglia. There have been some isolated records since 1960 but these are probably occasional migrants. The larvae feed on field bindweed and it probably disappeared due to the development of herbicides which reduced the abundance of its food plant.

The **short-haired bumblebee** *Bombus subterraneus* was formerly locally common across from Humberside to the south coast of England. It declined rapidly in the second half of the 20th century in conjunction with changing agricultural practices causing the loss of the diverse grasslands that provided the flowers they visited. The last British record was in Dungeness in 1988. It is found throughout Europe and into Asia as far west as Mongolia. It has also been deliberately introduced to New Zealand as a pollinator of red clover (in 1885 and 1906). The New Zealand bees were used in a reintroduction attempt in 2009 and 2010 but this failed, apparently because of a lack of genetic diversity in this stock. In 2012 another attempt at reintroduction was made using bees from Sweden. 51 queen bees were released at Dungeness, a further 49 the following year and 46 in 2014. The sighting of worker bees in 2013 confirmed that they had nested successfully.

Spotted-sulphur moth from Nemos 1895

Agricultural changes were only one factor contributing to the extinction of the **Essex emerald moth** *Thetidia smaragdaria*. This species is found from western Europe to Japan. The British population was last recorded along estuaries on the Essex and Kent coasts, with the last larvae found on the Essex saltings in 1991. The declining population had been monitored and a captive breeding programme established. The captive population survived until 1996 but died out. Attempts at reintroduction also failed. The larvae feed on sea wormwood. Unusually they are submerged by high tides. This makes them vulnerable to changes in coastal ecology. The decline of the species throughout its range is probably due to habitat changes resulting from changes in coastal grazing practices, removal of coastal vegetation and coastal development.

The most conspicuous of all grassland losses and reintroductions is the **great bustard** *Otis tarda*. This species has a range that extends from the Iberian peninsula and Morocco in the west to China in the east. It has been in decline since the early 19th century and its range is now highly fragmented. Some 50,000 birds remain, but the decline has been slowed by recent conservation action. In Spain, which holds half of the world's population, numbers have increased.

As such a large bird the bustard was an obvious game bird and was heavily hunted. By 1521 it was already something of a rarity in Britain as the Earl of Northumberland's Household Book of that year records that bustards were only to be taken "for my Lordes owne Mees [mess] at Prynicpall Feestes Ande noon on outher tyme Except my Lordes commaundment be otherwise."

Short haired bumblebee from Curtis 1924-39

Bustards were recorded from southern Scotland to Kent. The last Scottish record is from 1684 when Robert Sibbald reported it from East Lothian. They became extinct in Wiltshire in about 1810, Yorkshire and Lincolnshire by 1827 and Suffolk in 1832. The Game Act of 1831 restricted hunting of bustards to 1st September – 1st March, but by then it was far too late.

THE GREAT BUSTARD.*

(Otis Tarda, Linn.—*Outarde barbue*, Temm.)

Great bustard from Bewick 1804

British great bustards were hunted to extinction in the 1830s, with the last breeding in 1832 and the last two birds were killed in 1838 near Swaffham, Norfolk. Although changing agricultural practice probably contributed to their decline significant areas of suitable habitat remain, particularly in Wessex.

Since 1998 management of the species in Britain has been coordinated by the Great Bustard Group which aims to re-establish the species. Releases of young birds imported from Russia have taken place every year since 2004, with 20 birds each year released on Salisbury Plain. In the third year the first nest was found, but the eggs were infertile. The males reached maturity in the fifth year and the first chicks hatched in 2009.

Declines and extinctions in agricultural land continue today. The strange **wryneck** *Jynx torquilla* was widespread in central and south-east England, breeding in all English and Welsh counties except Cornwall and Northumberland. Since the 1830s it has been in decline. In 1954 there were 150-400 pairs in England, declining to fewer than 80 pairs in 1966, restricted to Kent and Surrey, and ceasing to breed after 1974. However, from 1969 Scandinavian migrants started breeding in Scotland, but in 1974 these ceased breeding as well. Only occasional breeding attempts have been recorded since then.

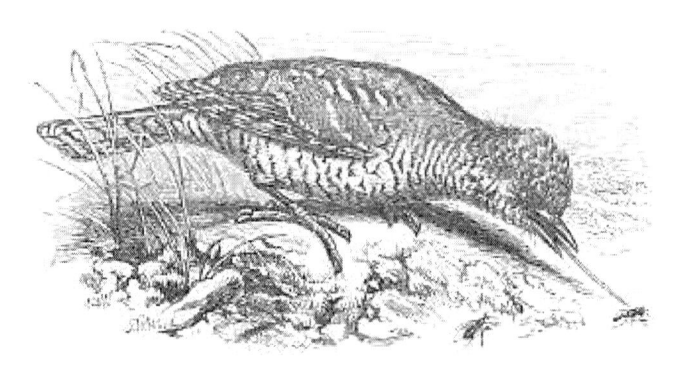

Wryneck from Wood 1869

The decline of the wryneck has been blamed on pesticides, habitat loss, competition for nest sites, climate change and predation. Pesticide use started after the decline had started. The cause of the decline in Britain and elsewhere in Europe is still not clear but a large decline seems to correlate with the agricultural depression in the 1920s resulting in neglected, ungrazed grasslands. The wryneck depends upon ants for a large part of its diet and it finds these easy to catch in well grazed grasslands.

The most recent bird to be lost as a breeding species in Britain was the **red-backed shrike** *Lanius collurio*, or 'butcher-bird'. These were familiar farmland predators until the mid 20th century. Agricultural change resulted in habitat loss, with clearance of hedgerows and intensive use of insecticides. As the birds became rarer egg collecting became more of a threat and declines were particularly rapid in the 1970s and 980s. The red-backed shrike became extinct as a British breeding species after 1992 when the last pair bred in Norfolk. However migrants still arrived on the south and east coast in small numbers and a pair tried to breed again in 2009. The first successful breeding was in 2010 and attempts have been regular since then. The numbers of breeding pairs remain extremely low.

Red-backed shrike from Wood 1869

Over the edge

Being surrounded by water the British Isles obviously have a very extensive coastline. Naturally much of this was marshland but a significant proportion was cliff. Cliffs provide a very special type of habitat, with exposed soil or rock faces, usually well drained and often subject to extreme weather. The habitats in these areas are varied and support distinct groups of animals.

By their very nature, cliffs are unstable environments and the species that live there are adapted to that instability. Not unreasonably human residents try to reduce that instability by shoring up cliffs, creating sea walls and other engineering works. These have radically altered the environments to the detriment of several species.

The **narrow Lixus weevil** *Lixus angustatus* was formerly quite common in the Fairlight district of East Sussex. It was last recorded in the dry undercliff of what is now the Hastings Country Park Nature Reserve in 1923 by R.S. Mitford. This species was not limited by its diet, feeding on such common species as a variety of thistle species. It was probably always a rare species, restricted to small patches of habitat, making it vulnerable to any development in these areas.

Narrow lixus weevil from Curtis 1924-39

The **carpenter bee** *Dufourea halictula* is a specialist associated with the flowers of sheep's-bit scabious, a localised plant of cliffs and escarpments of south-east England. British records were first made in 1910 at Horsell Common, Surrey. In 1913 it was found at nearby Byfleet and survived there until 1920. In 1948 it was present in Dorset, but was last seen there at Ferndown in 1953.

The small **cuckoo bee** *Nomada errans* was first collected in Britain in 1878 but not identified until 1944. It seems always to have been very localised on the Isle of Purbeck, Dorset, and has not been recorded since 1982. It is a scarce southern European species associated with chalk grassland with areas of open clay soil. This is essential for its survival as the clay is used as a nesting site by its host, the mining bee *Andrena nitidiuscula*. Its British site is soft-rock cliff and extinction at this site was probably due to deterioration of habitat caused by cliff stabilisation measures and by scrub encroachment on the grassland areas.

The largest of all cliff associated species ever recorded in Britain was the **white-tailed eagle** or **sea eagle** *Haliaetus albicilla*. These huge birds (with wings spans of up to 245 cm, or over 8 feet) were highly significant to ancient human populations in northern Britain. In Orkney the 3,000 year old 'Tomb of Eagles' contains bones of eight eagles and many tribes were thought to have left their dead to be eaten by birds of prey before burying their bones. In Shetland the fishermen thought that sea eagles ('Erne' or 'the soarer' in Anglo Saxon) drew fish up to the surface for them; unfortunately this led them to put eagle fat on

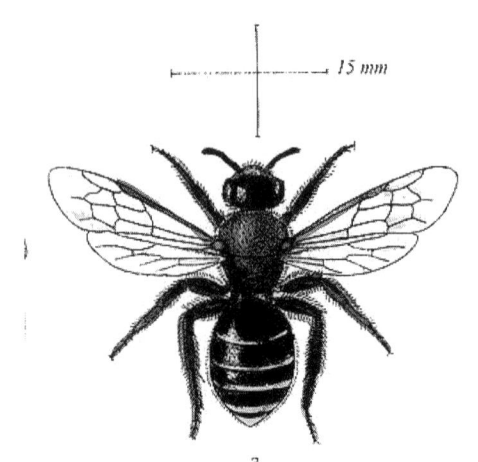

A *Dufourea* carpenter bee from Saunders 1896

their bait in the hope that it would help the catch. Early killing of sea eagles was limited and the birds bred throughout Britain until the 18th century: it has always been mainly a northern bird in Britain but there is a record of nesting on the Isle of Wight in 1780. They were killed by farmers and gamekeepers as predators and hunted for trophies and eggs collected. By 1800 they were restricted to Scotland and there only found in the north and west. They continued to decline as shooting estates continued to attempt to eliminate them through shooting and poisoning. They had died out on most of the mainland in the late 19th century. The Mull population was lost in the 1890s but may have survived on the Ardnamurchan peninsula until 1913. These would have been the last birds on the mainland. They bred on Rhum until 1907 and on Skye until 1916 when the last pair were killed by egg collectors. The last surviving British sea eagle was an albino female in the Shetland islands which was shot in 1918.

Sea eagles retained healthy breeding populations in Norway and young birds have been reintroduced to Britain from there. The first attempt was made in 1959 when two young birds were released at Glen Etive in Argyll. They adapted well but seemed too tame and were recaptured after attacking chickens. In 1968 the Royal Society for the Protection of Birds released four more on Fair Isle. These took to preying on fulmars, which became abundant in Scotland in the 20th century; three eagles died probably from becoming covered in the sticky oils that fulmars regurgitate when attacked, however, fulmars now form a significant part of the diet of the established eagles and fulmars decline wherever they are established.

More recent reintroductions by Scottish Natural Heritage and RSPB have been much more successful. These started in 1975 and between then and 1985 82 young eagles were released on Rhum. Most of these survived and settled on the island. In 1993 a five year release project started, resulting in the release of 58 eagles at Wester Ross on the mainland, and in 2007-12 on the east coast around the Firth of Tay and Forth where 20 birds were released. In 2007 releases also started in south-west Ireland.

Some of the birds from Rhum flew to Mull in the 1980s and the first nest there was seen in 1982. It took another three years before a pair successfully fledged a chick, since when breeding has taken place every year. There are now 16 pairs on Mull, which is probably the maximum the island can support. In 2012 there were 66 pairs in Scotland, rearing 60 chicks. The reintroduction has been very successful although not straightforward. Reintroduction has been hampered by the theft of eggs, which is combated by guarding initiatives such as Mull Eagle Watch.

Sea eagle from Thompson 1910

Although not a cliff dweller, the **Kentish plover** *Charadrius alexandrinus* is also limited to coastal areas, breeding on sand banks. It is a widespread species, breeding in the Americas, Europe and Asia. It has only ever been a localised breeding species in Britain. It was first recorded as a breeding species in Britain in 1787 at Sandwich in Kent, and later at other places along the Kent and Sussex coasts. Its rarity drew the attention of egg collectors and up until 1901 dogs were trained to hunt for the eggs. The drainage and disturbance of coastal marshes probably also contributed to its decline. By the 1880s it had become more restricted but was still common around Rye Harbour and Winchelsea. 'Hundreds' were reported to breed at Dungeness but these declined rapidly when this was publicised.

In 1905 the Royal Society for the Preservation of Birds employed a 'watcher' to protect the plovers from egg collectors and this was reported to be successful, with at least 21 pairs breeding successfully in that year, increasing to 44 pairs in 1906. However, it was only a temporary recovery and by the time the RSPB bought Romsey Marsh in 1931 the species was already extinct as a permanent breeding species.

They continue to visit Britain as migrants, in very small numbers, and there are occasional breeding attempts: Sussex in 1949-56, Suffolk 1952, and Lincolnshire 1979. They continued to breed in the Channel islands until 1975.

The most famous of all coastal cliff-associated extinct species is undoubtedly the **great auk** *Pinguinus impennis*. This was a large flightless seabird, being in effect the 'penguin of the north'. It has been hypothesised that the Welsh name for the species, 'pen gwyn' meant "white head", with similar names in Cornish and Breton. Whether this referred to the white patch on the bird's otherwise black head, or a white, guano-covered headland is disputed. Either way, it later gave rise to the word penguin. When explorers first encountered penguins in south polar waters they called them penguins, noting their superficial similarity to the northern hemisphere birds.

Great auks ranged around the northern Atlantic, from Canada to Norway, including Greenland, Iceland, the Faroe Islands, the British isles and France. In winter they migrated south, as far as Florida (although normally no further south than Massachusetts Bay) and Gibraltar. They foraged in shallow water on fish and crabs. They bred on rocky offshore islets, laying a single egg on the bare rock.

Populations probably numbered in the millions and fisherman were able to use the sight of large numbers of the birds on the sea as a marker for the Great Banks. There were probably only around 20 breeding colonies. By the early 19th

Great auk, painted by J.G. Keulmans around 1900

century the only breeding sites were on St. Kilda, Grimsey and Eldey islands near Iceland, and Funk island (the largest colony) and the Rochers-aux-Oiseau in Canada.

Humans hunted them from prehistoric times (100,000 years ago). A human skeleton buried in the Maritime Archai site at Port au Choix, Newfoundland in 2000BC was surrounded by at least 200 great auk beaks, which may be the remains of a cloak made from their skins. The Beothuk people of Newfoundland also made a pudding of their eggs. Although hunting led to the extinction of the great auk in the 1800s, ancient hunting had already had some serious impacts; in Greenland prehistoric hunting by the Saqqaq led to local declines.

In the 18th century the auks were killed for meat and oil by fishermen and whalers. There was also some hunting for feathers, the down feathers being used for stuffing pillows. Early explorers searching for the north-west passage used the auks as food and fishing bait. Later sailors were said to have run planks onto shore and herded hundreds of auks directly onto the ships for slaughter, although the reliability of this has been questioned. By the mid 16th century the European colonies had almost all been exterminated. Down collecting in the Americas did not become significant until after the eider ducks had been almost wiped out in the 1770s. The scale of the hunting was recognised as a serious issue as early as 1553 when the first attempts were made to protect some populations. In 1775 the representatives of Newfoundland petitioned Britain to halt the massacre of the birds but it took the government a further 19 years to ban killing the birds for feathers.

In 1794 Aaron Thomas of HMS Boston wrote of Funk island: "If you come for their Feathers you do not give yourself the trouble of killing them, but lay hold of one and pluck the best of the Feathers. You then turn the poor Penguin adrift, with his skin half naked and torn off, to perish at his leasure. This is not a very humane method but it is the common practize. While you abide on this island you are in the constant practize of horrid cruelties for you not only skin them Alive, but you burn them Alive also to cook their Bodies with. You take a kettle with you into which you put a Penguin or two, you kindle a fire under it, and this fire is absolutely made of the unfortunate Penguins themselves. Their bodys being oily soon produce a Flame; there is no wood on the island." They had disappeared from Funk island by 1800.

The last British one was seen on Stac an Armin, St Kilda in 1844. It was caught by three men from St Kilda who kept it alive for three days until a large storm broke over the island. Believing the bird was a witch responsible for the storm they beat it to death with sticks.

As the bird became rarer the demand for museum specimens increased and this played a significant role in the final extinction. The last breeding colony was at Gierfuglasker ("Great auk rock"), Iceland. The inaccessible cliffs of the island protected the colony but it was lost to a volcanic eruption in 1830. The colony moved to Eldey Island off south-western Iceland. When it was discovered in 1835 around 50 birds were present. They were exploited for museum skins and the last birds killed on 3rd July 1844. On that date Jón Brandsson and Sigurður Ísleifsson strangled the pair of adults and Ketill Ketilsson smashed the last egg. They were interviewed by John Wolley, a specialist on the auk and Ísleifsson told him that: "The rocks were covered with blackbirds [guillemots] and there were the Geirfugles [great auks] ... They walked slowly. Jón Brandsson crept up with his arms open. The bird that Jón got went into a corner but [mine] was going to the edge of the cliff. [I] caught it close to the edge – a precipice many fathoms deep. The black birds were flying off. I took him by the neck and he flapped his wings. He made no cry. I strangled him."

There was an apparently reliable claim of a single bird sighted on the Great Banks of Newfoundland in 1852, but since then there have been no sightings of this large distinctive bird.

The only illustration of a great auk drawn from life, a pet auk drawn by O. Worm in 1655

Urban sprawl

Heathlands are a particularly important habitat in the British isles. In pre-human times they probably had a restricted distribution, in areas that were too dry, too cold, or lacking in good soil for tree growth. The clearance of the great forests led to a significant increase in the extent of heathlands, although these were always in mosaics of different habitats, each heath being a comparatively small area.

In the early 1900s the heathlands of the south of England became the focus of development and sand extraction. The many animal species associated with these habitats declined, and the species with small populations became threatened with extinction. Many appear to have been lost all together.

The **mason wasp** *Odynerus reniformis* was recorded only from the heaths of Hampshire and Surrey. It was last recorded from the New Forest in 1909, although it survived in the Channel Islands until 1957. It nested in sand banks, including railway embankments. Nests have also been found in the walls of abandoned buildings. The cells of the nest were stocked with caterpillars, sawfly larvae and weevils. As many of the insects they hunt remain common, habitat loss is the most likely cause of the wasp's extinction in Britain.

The **square-spotted Melecta bee** *Melecta luctuosa* was found in the south of England until 1912. This bee is a parasite of another bee, *Anthophora retusa*. This host bee has also declined and this would have had a serious impact on its parasite. However, the square-spotted Melecta vanished while its host was apparently still common. It was probably changes in habitat affecting the adult stages that caused the decline. Once again this bee was last seen in the New Forest.

An *Odynerus* mason wasp from Curtis 1924-39

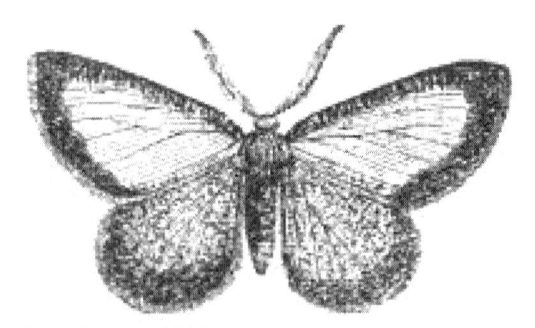

The frosted yellow from Newman 1869

The **frosted yellow moth** *Isturgia limbaria* was present in two widely separated regions: south-east England and in north-central Scotland. It was most frequently recorded near Stowmarket, Suffolk and also in East Anglia, Essex and Kent. It has not been seen since the last known occurrence at Stowmarket by Mr. Percy Reid in 1911. In its heyday there were two generations, flying in May/June and again in July/August. The larvae fed on broom growing on dry open embankments. The recorded localities were mostly close to estuaries and it may have been restricted to estuarine habitat with dry areas, although this is not the case for western European populations. Its decline was probably due to clearance of heathlands for housing and agriculture.

Enigmas and exceptional cases

Not all extinctions can be attributed to the simple extinction factors of hunting, agriculture, forestry or development. Some have disappeared for no very clear reason or for very specific reasons.

Unexplained extinctions include the **click beetle** *Selatosomus cruciatus* which was recorded only from around Windsor until 1839. The larvae feed on mare's tails plants in wet sandy soils, this is a common weed so it is hard to see why this beetle may have become extinct. It is a species of northern and eastern Europe and the British records were the most westerly for the species, they may therefore have been on the limits of the ecological preferences of the species and could be a natural extinction.

By the start of the 20th century a very obscure species seems to have vanished. The **fungus gnat** *Sciophila cliftoni* was known only from a single specimen found in Britain in the 1800s. There are no more records from the British isles but it has since been found to survive – in Russia. With no other information on the species it is impossible to explain its rarity.

Potter's Bar beetle *Aglyptinus agathidioides* is a mysterious species in the British fauna. It has been recorded only from two specimens found by the amateur beetle collector E.C. Bedwell in 1912. He found them in a moorhen's nest in Potter's Bar, near London. It was not named until 1931. This 1mm fungus beetle is easily overlooked but many coleopterists have searched for it in the nests of moorhens and other waterbirds. The closest relatives are from North American and it has been suggested that they may have been imported. How this may have come to be is not known and the record remains an enigma.

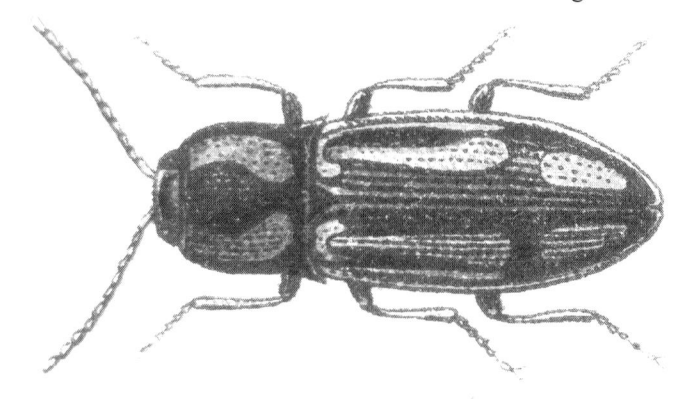

Selatosomus cruciatus click beetle from Reitter 1908

The **ground beetle** *Agonum chalconotum* (formerly *A. sahlbergii*) is an odd species to occur in Britain. Outside of the islands it is known only from Latvia, the northern European coast of Russia and from southern Siberia, northern Mongolia to Kazakhstan. It was first recorded in Britain in 1864 by a Mr. Bishop "in some numbers on the edge of a sandy bank on the north side of the Clyde a few yards west of Dunglass Castle". This was probably also the locality for specimens collected by Mr. Henderson a little later. This area of the Dunbartonshire coast was subsequently mostly modified and built upon and there are no subsequent records of the beetle in the area. They were next recorded in May 1909 on the coast of south Renfrewshire when a single specimen was found by J.E. Murphy. In 1914 he found two more a mile away from his earlier specimen, but there have been no further British records. It seems to have always been a rare species in the islands. It may be a relict species from the Ice Ages, dying out naturally. It is likely that coastal development accelerated its decline. However, many areas of suitable habitat remain and it is possibly that an overlooked population persists.

The **black-veined white butterfly** *Aporia crataegi* was first recorded from Britain in 1677. It was found in the south of England and south Wales, mainly in Kent, Hampshire, Gloucestershire and Sussex). Kent held the main populations, with 40 recorded colonies. It was always considered a rarity in Britain, despite being numerous in mainland Europe in isolated colonies that fluctuate in abundance. The last British colony died out in 1925. In Britain its food plants remain abundant; it has been suggested that it disappeared due to

Black veined white from Curtis 1924-39

disease, poor autumn weather with relatively mild winters and increased bird predation. It has been reintroduced into Fife, Scotland. This colony has been enabled to survive only by protecting the larvae from bird predation.

The **Isle of Wight wave moth** *Idaea humilata* became extinct in Britain around 1931. One further individual was recorded from Portsmouth, Hampshire in 1954, probably a migrant from Europe. The adult flies in a single generation in July, inhabiting grassy slopes by the sea. The food plant is unknown, although in captivity the larvae will feed on knotgrass, dandelion and dock. The cause of its extinction in Britain is not known as these plants are all common.

Ant nests often contain many strange insects, as well as ants. The **ant-living cylindrical bark beetle** *Myrmechixenus subterraneus* lived in ant-nests, feeding on fungi within the nests. Only two sites were known near Cromford in Derbyshire and the species was only found in 1956. What caused its disappearance is unknown, if it really is extinct.

The **clay groundling moth** *Nothris verbascella* was only recorded from Norwich in 1853 and Bury St. Edmunds in Suffolk in 1899. It was then found at Snettisham Carstone Quarry in Norfolk in 1967 where it remained present until 1971. The larva feeds on hoary mullein which is uncommon but is still present in the moth's last known site. It remains a widespread species in Europe and the cause of its extinction in Britain is not obvious.

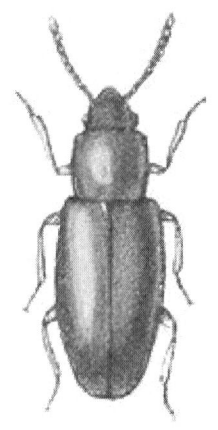

Ant-living bark beetle from Fowler 1889

A very odd extinction was the **brine shrimp** *Aremia salina*. This was found in the salt pans of Lymington in around 1740 and was first reported by M. Schlosser in 1775. In 1879 Edward King, mayor of Lymington, wrote: 'In this notice of our Salterns, we must not overlook a curious little creature that was found in them; and which has never been seen elsewhere, except in some salt-lakes of Siberia. It was known as The Lymington Brine Shrimp, and was first noticed by a Dr. Maty, about 1740. It lived in the brine tanks only, where no other creature could have existed, the concentrated salt-water being sufficient to destroy every marine organism. It was supposed, by the salt-makers, to cause a clearing of the brine; and was carefully transported to those vats which seemed to be deficient. It was never found in the evaporating pans, connected with the sea; but only in the deep store pits, which held the concentrated solution just before boiling.'

The British salt production industry declined in the 1800s and the last salt pan ceased operation in 1865. The brine shrimp has not been recorded subsequently. It remains widespread in North America and Europe.

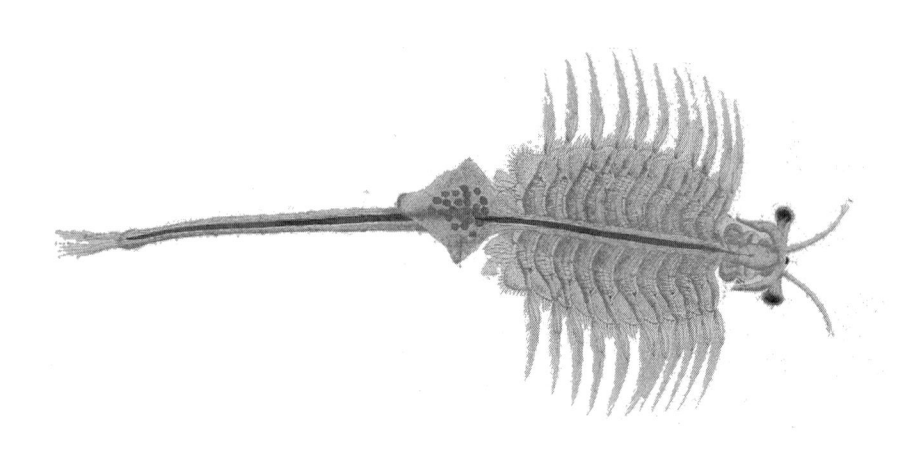

Brine shrimp from Joly 1840

The close association of some moths with specific larval food plants makes them vulnerable to extinction. This may be the case with the **lunar double-stripe moth** *Minucia lunaris* which was only known in Britain from two sites in Kent and East Sussex in the 1940s and 1950s. There are a few other records, but these seem to all be immigrant individuals. It was never common and was either a temporary colonisation or a rare species that declined with the reduction in its larval food plant, the oak tree. More clearly the **viper's bugloss moth** *Hadena irregularis* was probably lost due to the scarcity of its only British food plant, the Spanish catch-fly (despite the moth's common name). It was widespread in East Anglia and the London area until the 1960's when it became extinct, the last record being in 1969.

This specificity explains the extinction of one species very simply. The small tortoiseshell is one of the commonest British butterflies, but the **large tortoiseshell** *Nymphalis polychloros* has not been seen since 1953. Its larvae fed on elm leaves and its food source declined to near extinction due to the spread of Dutch elm disease in 1927. Dutch elm disease is caused by a fungus of the genus *Ophiostoma* which is spread by bark beetles. It was first identified in the Netherlands in 1921, hence its common name. The first invasion of the fungus had relatively little impact, but a more virulent form invaded in 1967. This

Large tortoiseshell from Shaw 1813

arrived in Britain in rock elm logs imported from North America. As a result of this virulent pathogen 25 million trees died in Britain, brining elm to the edge of extinction. The largest remaining population of elms in the islands is around Hove, near Brighton and it is possible that the large tortoiseshell could recolonise in this area.

In contrast to the simple explanation for the loss of the large tortoiseshell, the extinction of the **greater mouse-eared bat** *Myotis myotis* was far from simple. This is the only British bat species known to have been lost. It has declined throughout Europe due at least in part to loss of its roost sites and food sources. It catches its arthropod prey in flight (moths and cockroaches) but especially by gleaning off the ground where it catches crickets, beetles and spiders. Nursery roosts are in attics of buildings, and naturally would have been in caves. In Britain it was only known as a rare species of southern England, and was first recorded in 1958. Since its discovery it declined until only a few males were left in Sussex, and these disappeared after 1988. Some have been seen recently in Sussex and Dorset, but these are probably visitors from Europe. One was recorded hibernating in the winter of 2011-12. Their extinction was probably due to loss of roosting sites or disturbance and reduction in number of large beetles in the grasslands they foraged in, due to changed agricultural practices. In addition bats have faced a very particular problem: poisoning by the chemicals used in timber treatment in the attics so often used as nursery roosts.

Greater mouse eared bat by Specht from Brehms 1927

Some extinctions may perhaps have no simple explanation. The **burbot** *Lota lota* is a widespread freshwater fish, currently thought to be extinct in Britain although it used to occur in the Thames, Ouse, Esk, Skern, Swale, Tees, Derwent and Trent rivers. It was last caught in the river Cam in Cambridgeshire in 1969. In 2010 anglers reported catching burbot in Cambridgeshire and Cumbria, but these are not supported by specimens or photographs so its status remains uncertain. It is likely to have declined through the 20th century's heavy pollution of British waterways but may also have suffered from climatic changes. Unlike many of the declining or extinct species of Britain, the burbot was not a central-southern European species that found its northern limit in the islands, but rather a cold water fish approaching its southern limits. The warming climate may have contributed to its decline.

Of all species to be lost from the British fauna the most famous and the simplest to explain is the **grey wolf** *Canis lupus*. Well covered in historical record, literature and folklore the wolf was the only natives species to be deliberately exterminated.

Wolves were found throughout Britain and were abundant at times. Historical accounts show that wolves scavenged the corpses at the Battle of Hastings. Not surprisingly, these large, social predators were seen as a threat to humans and wildlife and were hunted to extinction.

Heavy hunting led to their relatively early decline in the south where there were many records of Anglo-Saxon wolf hunts. They had effectively disappeared from southern England as early as 800 AD, although a jaw bone from Kent has been dated to 1300 AD. In 942 AD the defeat of the Welsh King Idwal Foel ('the Bald') forced subsequent Kings of Aberffraw to pay a tribute to the English crown. Payment of this tribute lapsed and in 961 King Edgar invaded Wales in retaliation. In settling the peace the tribute was remitted and Edgar required instead an annual tribute of 300 wolf skins. Initially this was apparently no great hardship as the area around Offa's dyke teemed with wolves. After only four years though, the tribute could no longer be paid as there were no more wolves in the area. They did survive in north Wales, with a report of wolves around Holywell eating the corpses of soldiers after Henry II's invasion of Wales in 1165. In 1166 several deaths were attributed to a rabid wolf in Carmarthen.

Kings continued to exact tributes in the form of dead wolves: Edgar of England favouring wolf tongues and later Canute decreeing that "whoever kills any [wolves or foxes] is out of all danger of forfeiture". It was not until the 13th century that a systematic eradication campaign began. King Edward I placed a bounty on the wolf, aiming to have them completely exterminated from England

and Wales. In 1281 he commanded Peter Corbet to kill all the wolves of Gloucestershire, Worcestershire, Herefordshire, Shropshire and Staffordshire, but they were reputedly still present in the forests of Derbyshire in the 14th century (although this has been disputed). By 1485 wolves were largely restricted to Cumbria, the Pennines and Scotland.

Wolves survived in the greater space and isolation of Scotland until at least 1743, and in Ireland to 1786. Under King Alexander the Scottish wolf was just about the only large animal not reserved for the royal chase, and anyone could kill one. Laws encouraging wolf hunting were passed by James I in 1427, requiring three wolf hunts a year during the cubbing season. Although they remained plentiful in remote areas they were clearly in decline by this time. In 1563 Mary Queen of Scots took part in a hunt with 2,000 highlanders driving the woods of Athol, Mar and Badenoch. This yielded a reasonable head of 360 deer, but only five wolves.

In 1621 the bounty for a wolf in Sutherland stood at three shillings and four pence. Sutherland had a particularly strong aversion to wolves as during James VI's days the wolves of Sutherland dug up graves so often that the inhabitants of Eddrachillis took to burying their dead on the island of Handa. This was also practiced on Tanera Mòr and on Inishail. In Atholl coffins were made out of flagstones to keep out the wolves. This was close to the end for the species. The last wolf in the north-east of Scotland may have been the one killed in Kirkmichael Parish, Banffshire in 1644. However, Sutherland seems to have finally been cleared of wolves around 50 years later by a Mr. Polson.

The sound of a wolf howling long after their apparent extermination prompted a search. In the rugged land near Glen-Loth Polson, along with his young son and a herd boy, "discovered a narrow fissure in the midst of a confused mass of large fragments of rock, which, upon examination, he had reason to think might lead to a larger opening or cavern below, which the wolf might use as his den. Stones were now thrown down, and other means resorted to, to rouse any animal that might be lurking within. Northing formidable appearing, the two lads contrived to squeeze themselves through the fissure, that they might examine the interior, whilst Polson kept guard on the outside. The boys descended through the narrow passage into a small cavern, which was evidently a wolf's den, for the ground was covered with bones and horns of animals, feathers, and egg-shells, and the dark space was somewhat enlivened by five or six active wolf cubs. Not a little dubious of the event, the voice of the poor boys came up hollow and anxious from below, communicating this intelligence. Polson at once desired them to do their best, and to destroy the cubs. Soon after he heard the feeble howling of the whelps, as they were attacked below, and saw almost at the same time, to his great horror, a full-grown wolf, evidently the dam, raging furiously at the cries of her young, and now close upon the mouth of the cavern, which she had approached unobserved among the rocky inequalities of the place. She attempted to leap down, at one bound, from the spot where she was first seen: in this emergency, Polson instinctively threw himself forward on the wolf, and succeeded in catching a firm hold of the animal's long and bushy tail, just as the fore part of the body was within the narrow entrance of the cavern. He had, unluckily, placed his gun against a rock when aiding the boys in their descent, and could not now reach it. Without apprising the lads below of their imminent peril, the stout hunter kept a firm grip of the wolf's tail, which he wound round his left arm; and although the maddened brute scrambled, and twisted, and strove with all her might, to force herself down to the rescue of her cubs, Polson was just able, with the exertion of all his strength, to keep her from going forward. In the midst of this singular struggle, which passed in silence, - for the wolf was mute, and the hunter either from the engrossing nature of his exertions, or from his unwillingness to alarm the boys, spake not a word at the commencement of the conflict, - his son within the cave, finding the light excluded from above for so long a space, asked in Gaelic, and in an abrupt tone, "Father, what is keeping the light from us?" "If the root of the tail breaks," replied he, "you will soon know that." Before long, however, the man contrived to get hold of his hunting-knife, and stabbed the Wolf in the most vital parts he could reach. The enraged animal now attempted to turn and face her foe, but the hole was too narrow to allow of this; and when Polson saw his danger he squeezed her forward, keeping her jammed in, whilst he repeated his stabs as rapidly as he could, until the animal, being mortally wounded, was easily dragged back and finished." (Scrope 1838)

Given that the source of this story was writing more than 100 years after the event it may not be accurate. Even less likely is the reported sighting of a wolf in Sutherland in 1888. As reported by the Northern Times, September 26th, 1929 a guest of a shooting tenant lost his way on the moors and spent the night in a cave:

"I awoke with a great start and looked at my watch. It was one o'clock in the morning, and the weather had cleared. The moon appeared and the stars shone with a flickering and a frosty lustre like great diamonds on the black corsage of night. The musty odour had become most intense, and as my sleepy eyes threw off their shattered torpor, I saw with a shiver of apprehension a pair of sunken baleful looking eyes regarding me steadily and stealthily across the dying embers of the fire.

Grey wolf from Miller's 1859 'The British wolf-hunters A Tale of England in the Olden Time'

"I slipped a couple of cartridges into my gun, and as I did so I heard a low painful whine. I could now make out a white form like a huge dog lying not more than three feet from me. Its head rested on its paws and so far from showing any signs of hostility, it seemed to exhibit symptoms of friendliness. Its coat was a kind of silver-grey in colour and was thick and curly, but the face showed signs of great age.

"I stood up with my gun at my shoulder, but the beast did not move, and I could not find it in my heart to shoot; instead I threw it a ham sandwich. It nosed wearily, but did not attempt to eat it, so I tried it with a gorgonzola one, which it rejected with some evidence of repulsion. It then rose, and I saw to my unbounded astonishment that I was faced by a great silver-grey female wolf. She whined again, but kept her distance, and I then saw that in her eyes brooded a look of unutterable loneliness and misery.

"A female wolf, and the last wolf had been killed in Sutherland between 1690 and 1700. I could have gained lasting glory by shooting her, but my hand was stayed. It was I who had invaded her poor little dwelling, and she had shared it with me without hostility. She should suffer no harm from me. Her ancestors had wandered here when Scotland was joined to Greenland, and had shared these wan wastes with the majestic elk and the ivory-tusked boar; fighting and suffering and dying in those vast oak and pine forests, the remains of which are still visible in the great mosses which abound all over Sutherland."

Leaving aside these colourful stories, the last Scottish wolf is generally reputed to have been one killed by Sir Ewan Cameron of Locheil in at Killiecrankie, Lochaber in 1680, but a 'last' wolf was supposedly killed in 1743, although again some have called this a tall tale. This wolf was reputed to have killed two children crossing the hills from Cawdor. The Laird of Clan Mackintosh called a 'Tainchel', a drive to hunt the wolf. This start of the hunt was delayed by the late arrival of the legendary Highland deer stalker MacQueen of Pall a' Chrocain. The story goes that he was roundly abused for his late arrival but simply said 'What's the hurry?', lifted his plaid and drew out the head of the wolf. In 1830 Sir Thomas Dick Lauder recounted his words:

"As I came through the *slochd* [ravine] by east the hill there, I foregathered wi' the beast. My long dog there turned him. I bucked wi' him, and dirkit him, and syne whuttled his craig [cut his throat], and brought awa' his countenance for fear he might come alive again, for they are very precarious creatures."

How reliable any of this and whether this was indeed the last Scottish wolf are not known.

In Ireland wolves were blamed for the death of many people in 1420. In 1571 Kilmallock was attacked by the Clans Sweeny and Sheehy and left to wolves. They also swarmed over the aftermath of the battle of Bel-an-Chip in 1573. After the end of the Nine Years' War in 1603 wolves attacked the starving population. In the 1500s wolf skins were exported from Ireland and at least 100 a year were offloaded in Bristol (with a peak of 961 in one year). Attempts to eradicate the Irish wolves date from 1584. In that year John Perrot, Lord Deputy of Ireland ordered Robert Legge to draw up a plan of eradication. Bounties were offered throughout the 17th century but the wars occasioned by Oliver Cromwell's invasion of Ireland (1641-52) meant that conditions favoured the wolves. In 1652 the bounty had risen to £6 for a female, £5 for a male and less for young animals. A total of £3,847 5s was paid out between 1649 and 1656 and the wolf population was in decline. The last Irish wolf (and the last in the British isles) may have been the one killed near Mount Lenister in 1786.

As a final example, the strangest of all extinctions in Britain is the **St Kilda mouse** *Mus musuclus muralis.* This is an odd case as the mouse is not native to the British isles and yet this is an endemic, now extinct, subspecies, all of which sounds contradictory.

St Kilda mouse from the original description by Barrett-Hamilton 1899

Mice were introduced to Britain in early historical times, and may have been introduced to St. Kilda on the Viking longships that visited the island around 900AD. Since then they have adapted to the island's conditions and evolved into a sufficiently different form to be recognised as a different, newly evolved subspecies. This is bigger than the typical house mouse, as are the Faroese mouse populations which live in much the same environment and have a similar history. The relatively large size of the St. Kilda mouse enabled it to survive the cold conditions on the island. The mice were associated with the human settlers and depended upon them entirely for food. Due to its isolation and inhospitability people moved away from the island and it was completely evacuated in 1930. By 1938 the mouse had died out.

Rewilding – turning back the clock or tinkering?

In recent years there has been increasing talk of 'rewilding' - restoring sites to a more natural state by reintroducing the wild animals that once lived there. Species mentioned in this context often include wolves, lynx, bears and beavers. While these are tempting, romantic ideas, are they practical: could Britain's wild spaces be restored, and if so with what species?

Much of the densely populated British isles are clearly not a suitable home for free-ranging large predators like wolves and bears, but it has been suggested that the Scottish highlands could support viable populations of lynx and possible wolves. In terms of ecology this would be desirable, as at present these areas are occupied by un-naturally high populations of red deer. In the absence of any natural predator the deer have to be culled, and even then the damage to trees caused by deer over-population is severe. Wolves could restore some natural balance. The smaller lynx would not exercise the same degree of control, but in Europe they are also significant predators of deer. In an analysis of the practicality of reintroducing wolves it was concluded that wolves could be of benefit in reducing the need for culling the red deer population, and so avoiding some of the costs currently incurred by estate managers, although there would obviously be a cost in livestock losses. There was also more public support for the idea that might be expected. Even so it is hard to imagine a proposal to release wolves having a serious chance of receiving the political support it would need. A proposal to release wolves into a fenced estate in 1999 was rejected following opposition from sheep farmers. There is a proposal for lynx and this may well be more acceptable.

Of the other missing mammals wild boar have effectively reintroduce themselves by escaping from farms and experimental and accidental reintroductions of beavers have occurred. So the British isles are being rewilded, although not in any systematic way. Planned reintroductions have mainly been restricted to birds such as great bustards and white-tailed sea-eagles. The bustards have wide support but the sea-eagles have been highly contentious. It is clear that the idea of returning large predators has its problems, although arguably it is these predators that the ecosystem needs most.

Other species could be relatively straightforward, as long as the environmental conditions are suitable. As a survey of the range of extinct animals of Britain shows, the gaps in the British fauna are much wider than just wolves, lynx and large birds. Some of the smaller missing species have been returned: the pool frog, the short-haired bumblebee and, most famously, the **large blue butterfly** *Maculinea arion*. The large blue was naturally restricted to southern England where it was associated with chalk grassland. It was first recorded in 1795 and seems to have always been rare. By 1950 it was close to extinction, with only 25 sites left due to ploughing and forestry plantations. In 1972 there were only two sites left, although several others still appeared to be suitable.

Large blue from Humphreys & Westwood 1841.

These last two sites supported the wild thyme and the red ants that the butterflies depend upon. The eggs are laid on the thyme and the young caterpillars feed on the plants. The caterpillars exude a scent that induces the ants to pick them up and carry them into their nests. There they feed on the ant larvae. They are thus totally dependant on the presence of red ants. Although several red ant species were present in numerous sites, only the two occupied sites retained the particular red ant that the large blue needs. Each of these ant species has a very specific temperature requirement and ground temperature depends largely on vegetation height, so it turned out that the butterflies needed a very precise grass height. Changes in the pattern of sheep grazing and the decline of rabbit populations caused by myxomatosis changed the ground temperature and so eliminated the ants and the butterflies. The last two populations died out in 1979 and with them the British endemic subspecies *eutyphron* was lost. A different subspecies of the large blue was reintroduced to managed sites in 1984 using eggs from Sweden. This very carefully planned reintroduction has been highly successful: in 2006 there were an estimated 10,000 adult butterflies on 11 sites.

Although it would be perfectly practical to reintroduce some of the other invertebrate species lost from the British landscape there remains a possibility that small native populations may still survive, overlooked in some small patch of habitat. We can only be fully confident of the extinction of the larger, more conspicuous species – mostly the butterflies, some of the moths and some bees. Most of the invertebrates may also recolonise naturally if the habitat is suitable, as witnessed by the occasional sightings of visiting individuals of some of the moths and dragonflies. Effort and resources would probably be most effectively used in protecting and restoring habitats, rather than moving species. Where human intervention may be worthwhile is for species that cannot reach the islands on their own or which are likely to have played an important ecological role in the past.

Most of these ecological keystones, regulators and shapers are the large mammals at the centre of the rewilding debate. Even if it is thought desirable to return some of the larger animals to the landscape, this would not recreate a natural system. The British landscape has been modified by humans over thousands of years and has no natural stable state. In addition the changing climate means that all ecosystems are in a period of change. What is needed is not a return to a hypothetical wild past but the restoration of an ecosystem that can adapt to whatever the future holds. Reintroductions may play an important part in that. For example we may desire the return of beavers as wetland ecosystem engineers to recreate some degree of flood adaptability. We may wish to have wild boar back in our forests, disturbing the soil and dispersing seeds, helping to shift the forests from artificial monocultures to more natural, more adaptable mosaics. Recreating more natural, more dynamic ecosystems requires the return of the predators along with everything else, and moorland may be more in need of this than most habitats, probably being the most destabilised of all systems in Britain, but wolves will always remain the most difficult example.

With too many uncertainties and no original natural state to return to, rewilding Britain can never be a scientific programme. If it occurs, it will be as a series of separate experiments. Whilst rewilding would be scientifically fascinating, more importantly it would be romantic and inspiring.

List of extinct animals of the British Isles

The following species are probably extinct in the British isles, insects known from just single records are excluded as being of uncertain status. Species that have recolonised naturally are placed in parentheses, reintroductions are marked with the letter R.

brown bear *Ursus arctos*	10th century?
European beaver *Castor fiber*	1200 R
Eurasian lynx *Lynx lynx*	1250
wild boar *Sus scrofa*	1263 R
grey wolf *Canis lupus*	1786
capercaillie *Tetrao urogallus*	1769?
(**common crane** *Grus grus*	1800)
sawfly *Cimbex quadrimaculatus*	1800s
sawfly *Corynis crassicornis*	1800s
sawfly *Corynis obscura*	1800s
sawfly *Megalodontes cephalotes*	1800s
sawfly *Strongylogaster filicis*	1800s
longhorn beetle *Anoplodera virens*	1800s
longhorn beetle *Strangalia attenuata*	1800s
longhorn beetle *Plagionotus arcuatus*	1800s
fungus gnat *Sciophila cliftoni*	1800s
Manchester moth *Euclemensia woodiella*	1829
great bustard *Otis tarda*	1832 R
blue stag beetle *Platycerus caraboides*	1839
click beetle *Selatosomus cruciatus*	1839
false flower beetle *Scraptia dubia*	1842
great auk *Pinguinus impennis*	1844
longhorn beetle *Strangalia attenuate*	1845
Large copper *Lycena dispar*	1851
weevil *Bagous binodulus*	1861
click beetle *Cardiophorus gramineus*	1863
leaf beetle *Cryptocephalus violaceus*	1864
fungus beetle *Mycetophagus fulvicollis*	1870
pollen beetle *Meligenthes coracinus*	1873
many-lined moth *Costaconvexa polygrammata*	1875
chequer beetle *Tilloidea unifasciatus*	1877
brine shrimp *Aremia salina*	1879

reed tussock moth *Laelia coenosa*	1879
houting *Coregonus oxyrinchus*	1881
oil beetle *Meloe variegatus*	1882
black tern *Chlidonias niger*	1884
glow-worm *Lamprohiza splendidula*	1884
(**black-tailed godwit** *Limosa limosa*	1885)
Baillon's crake *Porzana pusilla*	1889
cuckoo bee *Coelioxys afra*	1892
(**northern goshawk** *Accipipter gentilis*	1893)
weevil *Bagous diglyptus*	1897
weevil *Lepyrus capucinus*	1897
weevil *Rhyncolus* (or *Phloeophagus*) *gracilis*	1897
speckled beauty moth *Faginovora arenaria*	1898
Blunt's flat-body moth *Depressaria depressana*	1900
(**leaf beetle** *Galeruca laticollia*	early 1900s)
caddis fly *Hydropsyche exocellata*	1901
longhorn beetle *Cerambyx scopolii*	1902
beetle *Hypocoprus latridioides*	1902
beetle *Philonthus confinis*	1902
whirligig beetle *Gyrinus natator*	1902
diving beetle *Rhantus aberratus*	1904
water beetle *Hydroporus aberrans*	1904
weevil *Lixus vilis*	1905
oil beetle *Meloe cicatricosus*	1906
(**gypsy moth** *Lymantria dispar*	1907)
capuchin beetle *Bostrichus capucinus*	1908
weevil *Ceutorhynchus hepaticus*	1909
weevil *Tychius polylineatus*	1909
mason wasp *Odynerus reniformis*	1909
chequered history beetle *Graphoderus bilineatus*	1910
frosted yellow moth *Isturgia limbaria*	1911
square-spotted Melecta bee *Melecta luctuosa*	1912
Potter's Bar beetle *Aglyptinus agathidioides*	1912
fen spider *Hypsosinga heri*	1912
diving beetle *Rhantus bistriatus*	1913
water beetle *Ochthebius aeneus*	1913
ground beetle *Agonum chalconotum*	1914
orache moth *Trachea atriplicis*	1915
white-tailed eagle or **sea eagle** *Haliaetus albicilla*	1918 R

flame brocade moth *Trigonophora flammea*	1919
narrow Lixus weevil *Lixus angustatus*	1923
dusky clearwing moth *Paranthrene tabaniformis*	1924
juniper bug *Chlorochroa juniperina*	1925
black-veined white butterfly *Aporia crataegi*	1925 R
grass spider *Mastigusa arietina*	1926
cylindrical bark beetle *Endophloeus markovichianus*	1927
reddish obrium longhorn beetle *Obrium cantharinum*	1929
beetle *Cardiophorus ruficollis*	1930
beetle *Trichodes apiarius*	1930
mining bee *Halictus maculatus*	1930
mining bee *Andrena nana*	1930
St Kilda mouse *Mus musuclus muralis*	1930
Kentish plover *Charadrius alexandrinus*	1931
marsh dagger moth *Acronicta strigosa*	1933
mining bee *Andrena polita*	1934
union rustic moth *Apamea pabulatricula*	1936
(small ranunculus moth *Hecatera dysodea*	1937)
blackthorn webworm moth *Dichomeris derasella*	1939
mining bee *Andrena floricola*	1939
mining bee *Eucera tuberculata*	1941
Cullum's bumblebee *Bombus cullumanus*	1941
mining bee *Andrena tridentata*	1944
mining bee *Andrena vaga*	1946
weevil *Ceratapion annatum*	1941
weevil *Otiorhynchus morio*	1941
orange-spotted emerald dragonfly *Oxygastra curtisii*	1946
minute seed moth *Borkhausenia minutella*	1950
digger wasp *Mellinus crabroneus*	around 1950
lunar double-stripe moth *Minucia lunaris*	1950s
oil beetle *Meloe autumnalis*	1952
bee *Andrena lepida*	1952
carpenter bee *Dufourea halictula*	1953
large tortoiseshell *Nymphalis polychloros*	1953
dainty damselfly *Coenagrion scitulum*	1953
two-tubercled orbweb spider *Gibbaranea bituberculata*	1954
Isle of Wight wave moth *Idaea humilata*	1954
ant-living bark beetle *Myrmechixenus subterraneus*	1956
water beetle *Sphercheus emarginatus*	1956

Norfolk damselfly *Coenagrion armatum*	1956
horned dung beetle *Platydema violaceum*	1957
weevil *Lixus paraplecticus*	1958
leaf beetle *Chrysomela tremula*	1958
(**conformist moth** *Lithophane furcifera*	1959)
spotted sulphur moth *Emmelia trabealis*	1960
Lewes wave moth *Scopula immorata*	1961
feathered ear moth *Pachetra sagittigera*	1963
burbot *Lota lota*	1969
viper's bugloss moth *Hadena irregularis*	1969
bee *Eucera nigrescens*	1970
clay groundling moth *Nothris verbascella*	1971
ground beetle *Pterostichus aterrimus*	1973
wryneck *Jynx torquilla*	1974
cudweed moth *Cucullia gnaphalii*	1979
large blue butterfly *Maculinea arion*	1979 R
great yellow bumblebee *Bombus distinguendus*	1981
cuckoo bee *Nomada errans*	1982
orange upperwing moth *Jodia croceago*	1983
Pashford pot beetle *Cryptocephalus exiguus*	1986
black-backed meadow ant *Formica pratensis*	1988
pool frog *Rana lessonae*	1995 R
short-haired bumblebee *Bombus subterraneus*	1988 R
greater mouse-eared bat *Myotis myotis*	1988
Essex emerald moth *Thetidia smaragdaria*	1991
(**red-backed shrike** *Lanius collurio*	1992)

Questionable records and possible introductions:
Bees *Andrena naula, Bombus pomorum, Chalicodoma ericetorum, Halictus subauratus, Hoplitis leucomelana, Hylaeus punctulatissima, Lasioglossum laeve, Megachile lapponica*
Beetles *Ampedus sanguineus, Anthrenus piminellae, Bagous arduus, Bagous petro, Ceutorhynchus syrites, Clytra laeviuscula, Coniocleonus hollbergi, Ebaeus pedicularis, Ebaeus pedicularius, Hister illigeri, Hister quadrinotatus, Hypera arundinis, Hypocassida subferruginea, Lepturobosca virens, Murmidius ovalis, Mycterus curculioides, Nephus bisignatus, Plagionotus arcuatus, Pleurophorus caesus, Rhynchites bacchus, Saprinus subnitescens, Tarsostenus univittatus* and *Trichodes alvearius*
Flies *Merodon clavipes*.

Butterflies *Argynnis niobe, Boloria dia, Chazara briseis, Iphicles podalirius*

Probable temporary colonisations
Bees: *Rhophites quinquespinosus*
Flies: *Rhaphium pectinatum, Dolichopus melanopus*
Moths: *Nola aerugula*
Butterflies: *Cyaniris semiargus*

References

Allen, A.A. 1970. Revisional notes on the British species of *Orthoperus* Steph. (Col., Corylophidae). *Entomologist's Record and Journal of Variation* **82**: 112-20

Allen, A.A. 1989. *Lamprohiza splendidula* (L.) (Col., Lamyridae) taken in Kent in 1884. *Entomologist's monthly magazine* **125**: 182

Allen, A.A. 1991. On *Bagous arduus* Sharp and *Bagous rudis* Sharp. Col Curculionidae. *Entomologist's Record and Journal of Variation* **104**: 199-201

Barrett-Hamilton, G.E.H. 1899. On species of the genus *Mus* inhabiting St. Kilda. *Proceedings of the Zoological Society of London.* (**1899**): 77-88.

Bees, Wasps & Ants Recording Society, 2013. *Anthophora retusa.* http://www.bwars.com/index.php?q=bee/apidae/anthophora-retusa.

Bewcik, T. 1804. *History of British Birds.* Longman, London.

Bloomfield, E.N. 1878. *Rhophites quinque-spinosus* and *Acronycta alni* near Hastings. *Entomologist's Monthly Magazine* **15**: 113

Brehms, A. 1927. *Brehms Tierleben.* 'Small' edition.

British Arachnologocial Society. 2014. Summary for *Mastigusa arietina* (Araneae). http://srs.britishspiders.org.uk/portal/p/Summary/s/Mastigusa+arietina

Brown, A. & P. Grice. 2005. *Birds in England.* Poyser, London.

Calwer, C.G. & G. Jager. 1876. Käferbuch. *Naturgeschichte der Käfer Europas. Zum Handgebrauche für Sammler.* Hoffmann, Stuttgart.

Carden, R.F. 2012. *Review of the Natural History of Wild Boar (Sus scrofa) on the island of Ireland.* Report for the Northern Ireland Environment Agency, Northern Ireland, UK, National Parks & Wildlife Service, Department of Arts, Heritage and the Gaeltacht, Dublin, Ireland and the National Museum of Ireland – Education & Outreach Department.

Carr, J.W. 1916. *The Invertebrate Fauna of Nottinghamshire.* Nottingham. J.& H. Bell Ltd.

Coggins, D. 1984. *The archaeology of early settlement in upper Teesdale, co. Durham.* MA Thesis, Durham University.

Collier, M. 1997: *Galeruca interrupta* sensu auct. Brit. Chrysomelidae rediscovered in Britain. *Coleopterist* **53**: 93

Collins, N.M. & J.A. Thomas (eds.) 1991. *The Conservation of Insects and Their Habitats.* Academic Press, London.

Conroy, J.W.H. & A.C. Kitchener. 1996. The Eurasian beaver (*Castor fiber*) in Scotland: a review of the literature and historical evidence. *Scottish Natural Heritage Review* **49**

Cooter, J. 1991. In: *A Coleopterist's Handbook*, ed. 3. The Amateur Entomologists' Society, Feltham.

Cuming, N. 2006. The discovery of *Rhynchites auratus* (Scopoli) (Coleoptera: Rhynchitidae), a species new to Essex, and previously considered extinct in Britain. *Essex Naturalist* **23**: 36-37

Curtis, J. 1824-39. *British Entomology, being illustrations and descriptions of the genera of insects found in Great Britain and Ireland; containing coloured figures from nature of the most rare and beautiful species, and in many instances of the plants upon which they are found.* London.

Dale, C.W. 1878. *The history of Glanville's Wootton, in the county of Dorset, including its zoology and botany.* Hatchards, London.

Dobson, R.M. & E.G. Hancock. 2008. Historical review of a cabinet of Coleoptera from Thomas George Bishop's collection connected with James Francis Stephens. *Glasgow Naturalist* **25**: 9-14

Donisthorpe, H.St.J.K. 1939. *A Preliminary List of the Coleoptera of Windsor Forest.* N. Lloyd and Co., London.

Duffey, E. 1977. The re-establishment of the large copper butterfly *Lycaena dispar batava* on Woodwalton Fen National Nature Reserve, Cambridgeshire, England, 1969-73. *Biological Conservation* **12**: 143-158

Elton, C.S. 1966. *The Pattern of Animal Communities.* Methuen and Co. Ltd., London.

Emerson, P.H. 1887. *Life in Field and Fen.* Bell & Sons, London

Eversham, B.C. 1999. Scarabaeidae: Psammobiini imported into Cambridgeshire. *Br. Journ. Entomol. Nat. Hist.* **12**: 33

Falk, S. 1991. A review of the scarce and threatened bees, wasps and ants of Great Britain. *Research and Survey in Nature Conservation*, Peterborough.

Falk, S.J. & P. Chandler. 2005. *A review of the scarce and threatened flies of Great Britain. 2. Nematocera and Aschiza.* JNCC.

Falk, S.J. & P. Chandler. 2005. *A review of the scarce and threatened flies of Great Britain. 3. Empididoidea.* JNCC.

Fittis, R.S. 1891. *Sports and pastimes of Scotland historically illustrated.* A. Gardner, London.

Fleming, R. 1998. Domesday Book and the Law: Society and Legal Custom in Early Medieval England. Cambridge University Press, Cambridge.

Forster, G.N. 2010. *A review of the scarce and threatened Coleoptera of Great Britain. Part 3: Water Beetles.* JNCC.

Fowler, W.W. 1889. *The Coleoptera of the British islands: a descriptive account of the families, genera, and species indigenous to Great Britain and Ireland, with notes as to localities, habitats, etc.* Reeve & Co., London.

Gleed-Owen, C.P. 2000. Subfossil records of *Rana* cf. *lessonae, Rana arvalis* and *Rana* cf. *dalmatina* from Middle Saxon (c. 600-950 AD) deposits in eastern England: evidence for native status. *Amphibia-Reptilia* **21**: 57-65

Goldsmith, O. 1865. *A History of the Earth and Animated Nature.* Lippincott, Philadelphia.

Hampshire Records Office. http://apps.nationalarchives.gov.uk/a2a/records.aspx?cat=041-mildmay&cid=5-4-4-1#5-4-4-1

Heath, J. & Emmet, A.M. (Eds.) 1983. *The Moths and Butterflies of Great Britain and Ireland, Vol.* **10**. Harley Books, New York.

Hetherington, D.A., Lord, T.C. & Jacobi, R.M. 2005. New evidence for the occurrence of Eurasian lynx (*Lynx lynx*) in medieval Britain. *Journal of Quaternary Science* **21**: 3-8.

Hodge, P.J. & Jones, R.A. 1995. *New British Beetles: Species Not in Joy's Practical Handbook,* British Entomological & Natural History Society, Reading.

Holloway, S. 1996. *The Historical Atlas of Breeding Birds in Britain and Ireland 1875-1900.* T. & A.D. Poyser, London.

Humphreys, H.N. & J.O. Westwood. 1841. British butterflies and their transformations: arranged and illustrated in a series of plates by H.N. Humphreys; with characters and descriptions by *J.O. Westwood.* W. Smith, London.

Hyman, P. S. (revised Parsons, M.S.) 1992. *A review of the scarce and threatened Coleoptera of Great Britain. Part 1.* U.K. Nature Conservation: 3. Peterborough: Joint Nature Conservation Committee.

JNCC. 2010. UK Priority Species data collation *Harpalus honestus* version 2. http://jncc.defra.gov.uk/_speciespages/ 2310.pdf

Johnstonus, J. 1678. *A Description of the Nature of Four-Footed Beasts with their Figures Engraven in Brass.*

Joly, N. 1840. *Histoire d'un petit crustacé (*Artemia salina*, Leach), auquel on a faussement attribué la coloration en rouge des marais salans méditerranéens; suivie de recherches sur la cause réele de cette coloration.* Boehm, Montpellier.

Jones, J. (ed.) 1816. *Encyclopaedia Londiniensis.* Vol **15**.

Joy, N.H. 1932. *A Practical Handbook of British Beetles.* H.F. & G. Witherby, London.

Kitchener, A.C. & J.W.H. Conroy. 1997. The history of the Eurasian Beaver *Castor fiber* in Scotland. *Mammal. Rev.* **27**(2): 95-108

Lauder, Sir T.R. 1830. *Account of the Moray Floods of August, 1829.*

Levey, B. 1997. *Meligethes corvinus* Erichson, 1845 (Coleoptera: Nitidulidae) reaffirmed as a British species. *British Journal of Entomology and Natural History* **10**: 7-8

Lindroth, C.H. 1960. On *Agonum sahlbergi* Chd. (Col., Carabidae). *Entomologist's Monthly Magazine* **96**: 44–47.

Liston A, Knight G, Sheppard D, Broad G, Livermore L (2014) Checklist of British and Irish Hymenoptera - Sawflies, 'Symphyta'. *Biodiversity Data Journal* **2**: e1168. doi: 10.3897/BDJ.2.e1168

Logunov, D.V. 2011. Where are you from, the Manchester Moth? *Micro Miscellanea, Newsletters of the Manchester Microscopical & Natural History Society* **78**: 10-12

Lovegrove, R. 2007. *Silent Fields: The long decline of a nation's wildlife.* Oxford University Press, Oxford

Lynch, A.H., J. Hamilton & R.E.M. Hedges. 2008. Where the wild things are: aurochs and cattle in England. *Antiquity* **82**: 1025-1039

Miller, T. 1859. *The British wolf-hunters. A Tale of England in the Olden Time.* Routledge, London.

Morris, F.O. 1850-1857. *History of British Birds.* Groombridge & Sons, London.

Morris, F.O. 1853. *A History of British Butterflies.* Groombridge & Sons, London

Morris M.G. 1998. Continental examples of some extinct, very rare, erroneous, dubious and possibly fraudulent British weevils (Coleoptera, Curculionoidea). *Br. J. Ent. Nat. Hist.* **11**: 109 Reitter, E. 1908-17. *Fauna Germanica - Die Käfer des Deutschen Reiches.* Lutz, Stuttgart

Murphy, J.E. 1918. Re-occurrence of *Anchomenus* (*Agonum*) *sahlbergi* Chaud. In Scotland. *Entomologist's Monthly Magazine* **54**: 33-34.

Natural England 2014. *Natural England Commissioned Report 18. A review of the scarce and threatened beetles of Great Britain. The darkling beetles and their allies Aderidae, Anthicidae, Colydiidae, Melandryidae, Meloidae, Mordellidae, Mycetophagidae, Mycteridae, Oedemeridae, Pyrochroidae, Pythidae, Ripiphoridae, Salpingidae, Scraptiidae, Tenebrionidae & Tetratomidae (Tenebrionoidea less Ciidae)*

Nelson, T.H. 1907. *The birds of Yorkshire. Being a historical account of the avifauna of the county.* A. Brown, London.

Nemos, F. 1895. *Europas bekannteste Schmetterlinge. Beschreibung der wichtigsten Arten und Anleitung zur Kenntnis und zum Sammeln der Schmetterlinge und Raupen.* Oestergaard Verlag, Berlin.

Newman, E. 1869. *An illustrated natural history of British moths.*

Newport, G. 1851. *On the Natural History, Anatomy and Development of the Oil Beetle,* Meloe, *more especially of* Meloe cicatricosus, *Leach.* R. Taylor, London.

Newton, A.C. 2010. Biodiversity in the New Forest. Pisces Publications, Newbury

Netherstole-Thompson, D. & M. Netherstole-Thompson. 1986. *Waders: their breeding, haunts and watchers.* Poyser, London.

Nilsen, E.B., E.J. Milner-Gulland, L. Schofield, A. Mysterud, N.C. Stenseth & T. Coulson. 2007. Wolf reintroduction to Scotland: public attitudes and consequences for red deer management. *Proceedings of the Royal Society B* **274**: 995-1003

Olsen, L.H., Sunesen, J. & Pedersen, B.V. 2001. *Small Woodland Creatures*, Oxford University Press, Oxford

Palacin, C. & J.C. Alonso 2008. An updated estimate of the world status and population trends of the Great Bustard. *Ardeola* **55**:13-25.

Ritchie, J. 1920. *The Influence of Man on Animal Life in Scotland.* Cambridge University Press, Cambridge

Saunders, E. 1896. *The Hymenoptera Aculeata of the British Islands. A descriptive account of the families, genera, and species indigenous to Great Britain and Ireland, with notes as to habits, localities, habitats, etc.* London.

Sharrock, J.T.R. 1986. *The Atlas of Breeding Birds in Britain and Ireland.* BTO.

Shaw, G. 1813. *The naturalists' miscellany: or coloured figures of natural objects; drawn and described immediately from nature.* Nodder & Co., London.

Shirt, B.D. (ed.) 1987. *British Red Data Books 2. Insects.* Peterborough.

Skinner, B. 1998. *The Colour Identification Guide to Moths of the British Isles, Second Edition.* Viking.

Smith, C. 2000. A grumpie in the sty: an archaeological view of pigs in Scotland, from their earliest domestication to the agricultural revolution. *Proceedings of the Society of Antiquarists of Scotland* **130**: 705-724

South, R. 1907. *The Moths of the British Isles.* Wartne & Co., London

Strudwick, T. 2008. A survey of *Odynerus simillimus* nest sites in the Norfolk Broads in 2008. http://hymettus.org.uk/downloads/O.%20simillimus%20in%20Norfolk%2008.pdf

Stuart, J.S. & C.E. Stuart. 1848. *Lays of the deer forest: with sketches of olden and modern deer-hunting; traits of natural history in the forest, traditions of the clans; miscellaneous notes.* Vol. 2.

Telfer, M.G. 2014. Carabid GB provisional Red List 2014. *Scybalicus oblongiusculus.* http://carabidredlist.blogspot.co.uk/2014/03/scybalicus-oblongiusculus.html

Thomson, A.L. 1910. *Britain's Birds and their Nests.* Chambers, London

Ticehurst, N.F. 1909. *A history of the birds of Kent.* Witherby & Co., London.

Tilbury, C., Williams, D., Jukes, M. & Straw, N. 2010 The re-establishment of gypsy moth *Lymantria dispar*(Linn.) in the UK. *Atropos*, **40**, 36-42.

Twinn, P.F.G. & P.T. Harding. 1999. *Provisional atlas of the longhorn beetles (Coleoptera: Cerambycidae) of Britain.* Biological Records Centre, Huntingdon.

Verrall, G.H. 1901. *British Flies, vol. 3: Platypezidae, Pipunculidae, Syrphidae of Great Britain:* 17-121 (Catalogue); 127-691.

Westwwod, J. 1840 'British butterflies and their transformations: arrange and illustrated in a series of plates by H.N. Humphreys; with characters and descriptions by J.O. Westwood. W. Smith, London

Wheeler, A. 1969. *The Fishes of the British Isles and North West Europe.* Macmillan.

Williams, P.H., A. Byvaltsev, C. Sheffield, P. Rasmont. 2012. *Bombus cullumanus* – an extinct European bumblebee species? *Apidologie* **44**: 121-132

Wood, J.G. 1869. *Illustrated Natural history.* Routledge & Sons, London

Yalden, D. 1999. *The history of the British mammals.* Poyser, London.

Young, M. 1997. *The Natural History of Moths.* Poyser, London.

Zilli, A., L. Ronkay & M. Fibiger. 2005. *Noctuidae Europaeae* Vol. **8**: 1-32

Index

Accipipter gentilis - 24, 80
Acronicta strigosa - 80
Aglyptinus agathidioides - 61, 80
Agonum chalconotum - 62, 80
Apamea pabulatricula - 21, 81
Acronicta strigosa - 43, 81
Ampedus sanguineus - 82
Andrena - 43, 81-82; *floricola* 43, 81; *lepida* 81; *nana* 43, 81; *naula* 82; *polita* 43, 81; *tridentata* 43, 81; *vaga* 81
Anoplodera virens - 79
ant, black-backed meadow - 82
Anthrenus piminellae - 82
Aporia crataegi - 62, 81
Argynnis niobe - 7, 83
Aremia salina - 64, 79
auk, great - 54-57, 79
aurochs - 6-7, 79
Bagous - 30, 42, 79, 82; *arduus* 82; *binodulus* 30, 79; *diglyptus* 42, 80; *petro* 82
bat, greater mouse-eared - 66, 82
bear – 15-17, 75, 79
beaver - 37-38, 75, 79
bee - 40, 43, 45-46, 51, 59, 80-82; bumblebee 40, 43, 45-46, 81-82; carpenter 51, 81; cuckoo 51, 80, 82; Melecta 59, 80; mining 43, 81
beetle - 9, 17-18, 20, 30-33, 39-42, 44, 50, 61, 63, 79-82; bark 21, 63, 72, 79; blister 9; capuchin 20, 80; chequer 41, 79; history 30, 80; click 61, 79; diving 30,32, 80; dung 82; ground 62, 80, 82; false flower 18, 79; fungus 79; glow-worm 42, 80; leaf 39, 44, 79-80, 82; longhorn 17-18, 20, 79-80, 81; oil 40, 80-81; pollen 30, 32, 80; pot 33, 82; Potter's Bar 61, 80; stag 17, 79; water 28-31, 80-81; weevil 30, 39-40, 42, 50, 79-81; whirligig 32, 80
boar - 23-24, 75, 79
brine shrimp - 64, 79
Boloria dia - 7, 83
Bombus - 40, 43, 45-46, 81-82; *cullumanus* 40, 81; *distinguendus* 43, 82; *pomorum* 82; *subterraneus* 45-46, 82
Borkhausenia minutella - 44, 81
Bos primigenius - 6-7, 79
Bostrichus capucinus - 20, 80

bug, juniper - 23, 81
burbot - 67, 82
bustard - 46-48, 79
butterfly - 7, 28-30, 62, 65, 75-77, 79, 81-83; black-veined white 62, 81; large blue butterfly 75-77, 82; large tortoiseshell 65, 81; Niobe fritillary 7, 83; Weaver's fritillary 7, 83; hermit 7, 83; Large copper 28-30, 79; scarce swallowtail 7, 83
caddis fly - 80
capercaillie - 11-13, 79
crane - 27, 79
crake, Baillon's - 37, 80
Canis lupus - 67-72, 75, 79
Cardiophorus - 79, 81; *gramineus* 79; *ruficollis* 81
Castor fiber - 37-38, 75, 79
Cerambyx scopolii - 80
Ceratapion annatum - 81
Ceutorhynchus - 39, 80, 82; *hepaticus* 39, 80; *syrites* 82
Chalicodoma ericetorum - 82
Charadrius alexandrinus - 54, 81
Chazara briseis - 7, 83
Chlidonias niger - 35-36, 80
Chlorochroa juniperina - 23, 81
Chrysomela tremula - 44, 82
Cimbex quadrimaculatus - 7, 79
Clytra – 6; *laeviuscula* 6; *quadripunctata* 6
Coelioxys afra - 80
Coenagrion - 33-34, 81-82; *armatum* 33, 82; *scitulum* 32-34, 81
Coniocleonus hollbergi - 82
Coregonus oxyrinchus - 80
Corynis - 7, 79; *crassicornis* 7, 79; *obscura* 7, 79
Costaconvexa polygrammata - 30, 79
Cryptocephalus - 33, 39, 79, 82; *exiguus* 33, 82; *violaceus* 39, 79
Cucullia gnaphalii - 22, 82
Cyaniris semiargus - 83
damselfly - 33-34, 81-82; dainty 33-34, 81; Norfolk 33, 82
Depressaria depressana - 42, 80
Dichomeris derasella - 43, 81
Dolichopus melanopus - 83
dragonfly, orange-spotted emerald - 33, 81

Dufourea halictula - 51, 81
eagle, white-tailed or sea - 51-53, 80
Ebaeus pedicularius - 82
Emmelia trabealis - 45, 82
Endophloeus markovichianus - 20, 81
Eucera - 43, 81-82; *nigrescens* 82; *tuberculata* 43, 81
Euclemensia woodiella - 18-19, 79
Faginovora arenaria - 21, 80
Formica pratensis - 82
frog, pool - 35, 82
fungus gnat - 61, 79
Galeruca laticollia - 80
Galerula laticollis - 8
Gibbaranea bituberculata - 23, 81
godwit, black-tailed - 29, 80
goshawk, northern - 24, 80
Graphoderus bilineatus - 30, 80
Grus grus - 27, 79
Gyrinus natator - 32, 80
Hadena irregularis - 65, 82
Haliaetus albicilla - 51-53, 80
Halictus - 43, 81-82; *maculatus* 43, 81; *subauratus* 82
Hecatera dysodea - 9, 81
Hister – 82; *illigeri* 82; *quadrinotatus* 82
Hoplitis leucomelana - 82
houting - 80
Hydropsyche exocellata - 80
Hydroporus aberrans - 30, 80
Hylaeus punctulatissima - 82
Hypera arundinis - 82
Hypocassida subferruginea - 82
Hypocoprus latridioides - 80
Hypsosinga heri - 30, 80
Idaea humilata - 63, 81
Iphicles podalirius - 7, 83
Isturgia limbaria - 60, 80
Jodia croceago - 22, 82
Jynx torquilla - 48-49, 82
Laelia coenosa - 30, 80

Lamprohiza splendidula - 42, 80
Lanius collurio - 49, 82
Lasioglossum leave - 82
Lepyrus capucinus - 80
Lepturobosca virens - 82
Limosa limosa - 29, 80
Lithophane furcifera - 22, 82
Lixus - 40, 50, 81-82; *angustatus* 50, 81; *paraplecticus* 82; *vilis* 40, 80
Lota lota - 67, 82
Lycena dispar - 26-30, 79
Lymantria dispar - 21, 80
lynx - 11, 75, 79
Maculinea arion - 75-77, 82
Mastigusa arietina - 81
Megachile lapponica - 82
Megalodontes cephalotes - 7, 79
Melecta luctuosa - 59, 80
Meligenthes coracinus - 79
Mellinus crabroneus - 81
Meloe - 40-41, 80-81; *autumnalis* 40, 81; *cicatricosus* 40, 80; *mediterraneus* 41; *variegatus* 40, 80
Merodon clavipes - 82
Minucia lunaris - 65, 81
moth - 9, 18-19, 21-22, 30, 40, 42-46, 60, 63, 65, 79-82; blackthorn webworm moth 43, 81; Blunt's flat-body 42, 80; clay groundling 63, 82; conformist 22, 82; cudweed 22, 82; dusky clearwing 22, 81; Essex emerald 46, 82; feathered ear 40, 82; flame brocade 21, 81; frosted yellow 60, 80; gypsy 21, 80; Isle of Wight wave 63, 81; Lewes wave 40, 82; lunar double-stripe 65, 81; Manchester 18-19, 79; many-lined 30, 79; marsh dagger 43, 80; minute seed 44, 80; orache moth 30, 80; orange upperwing 22, 82; reed tussock 30, 80; small ranunculus 9, 81; speckled beauty 21, 80; spotted sulphur 45, 82; union rustic 21, 81; viper's bugloss 65, 82
mouse, St Kilda - 72-73, 81
Murmidius ovalis - 82
Mus musuclus muralis - 72-73, 81
Mycetophagus fulvicollis - 79
Mycterus curculioides - 82
Myotis myotis - 66, 82

Myrmechixenus subterraneus - 63, 72
Nephus bisignatus - 82
Nola aerugula - 83
Nomada errans - 51, 82
Nothris verbascella - 63, 82
Nymphalis polychloros - 65, 81
Obrium cantharinum - 20, 81
Ochthebius aeneus - 31, 80
Odynerus reniformis - 59, 80
Otiorhynchus morio - 81
Otis tarda - 46-48, 79
Oxygastra curtisii - 33, 81
Pachetra sagittigera - 40, 82
Paranthrene tabaniformis - 22, 81
Philomachus pugnax - 28
Philonthus confinis - 80
Phloeophagus gracilis see *Rhyncolus gracilis*
Pinguinus impennis - 54-57, 79
Plagionotus arcuatus - 79, 82
Platalea leucorodia - 28
Platycerus caraboides - 17, 79
Platydema violaceum - 82
Pleurophorus caesus - 7, 82
plover, Kentish - 54, 81
Pterostichus aterrimus - 82
Porzana pusilla - 37, 80
Rana lessonae - 35, 82
Rhantus - 30, 32, 80; *aberratus* 30, 80; *bistriatus* 32, 80
Rhaphium pectinatum - 83
Rhophites quinquespinosus - 83
Rhynchites bacchus - 82
Rhyncolus gracilis - 42, 80
ruff - 28
Saprinus subnitescens - 82
sawfly - 7, 79
Sciophila cliftoni - 61, 79
Scopula immorata - 40, 82
Scraptia dubia - 18, 79
Scybalicus oblongiusculus - 9

Selatosomus cruciatus - 61, 79
shrike, red-backed - 49, 82
Sitaris muralis - 9
Sphercheus emarginatus - 30, 81
spider - 23, 30, 80-81; fen 30, 81; grass 81; two-tubercled orbweb 23, 81
spoonbill - 28
Strangalia attenuate - 17-18, 79
Strongylogaster filicis - 7, 79
Sus scrofa - 23-24, 75, 79
Tarsostenus univittatus - 82
tern, black - 35-36, 80
Tetrao urogallus - 11-13, 79
Thetidia smaragdaria - 46, 82
Tilloidea unifasciatus - 41, 79
Trachea atriplicis - 30, 80
Trichodes - 81-82; *alvearius* 82; *apiarius* 81
Trigonophora flammea - 21, 81
Tychius polylineatus - 39, 80
Ursus arctos - 13-15, 75, 79
wasp - 59, 80-81; digger 81; mason 59, 80
wryneck 48-49, 82
wolf - 67-72, 75, 79